The Witchfinder and the Devil's Darlings

Simon Peters

Lucas Books

www.lucasbooks.co.uk

The Witchfinder and the Devil's Darlings

Simon Peters

© Copyright 2003

First Published by
LUCAS BOOKS 2003

ISBN 1903797-21-7

British Library Cataloguing in Publication Data
A catalogue record for this book is available from the british library

Printed in the UK by Brackenbury Associates – Ipswich

Contents

Illustrations

A King, a Judge and the Witchfinder-General

Three men – one a king, one a judge and one a ruthless witch-hunter. Three men of very different class and character. Three men whose lives spanned almost 150 years, and each one of them an important figure in the grim story of English witchcraft. The king was James I of England [James VI of Scotland]. Born in Edinburgh Castle in the summer of 1566, he was only a few months old when his father was murdered, and little more than a year old when his mother, Mary Queen of Scots, was forced to abdicate in his favour.

Young James grew up in turbulent times. He was kidnapped by nobles and survived several plots to kill him, one supposedly concocted by a gang of Scottish witches. And later and more famously, there was that plot against him involving Guy Fawkes. James was conceited, lazy and contemptuous of women, and when he became King of England in 1603 he presided over a royal court that was corrupt and degenerate beyond the norm.

It was also a time when most people believed in witches and their devilish powers. At first James shared that view with an uncommon passion, even to the point of taking a close interest in the conduct of the trials of Scottish and English witches. He even went so far as to declare that those who doubted the reality of witchcraft were probably witches themselves. Indeed, he considered himself such an expert on witchery that an influential book on the subject was issued under his name.

Within months of gaining the English throne he tightened up the witchcraft laws of his new realm to bring them more into line with the harsher regime that existed in Scotland. Death became mandatory, although in some categories it was at the second offence, and the idea that witchcraft involved a pact with the Devil and the keeping of imps was given new emphasis in English law. Thankfully for those English men and women who had the misfortune to be indicted under King James's new laws, the barbarous tortures used in Scotland and execution by burning [usually preceded by the mercy of garrotting] remained north of the border. English witches were executed by hanging which was really a form of strangulation. Two or three were burned at the stake but that was because their offences of witchery had been mixed up with the old feudal crime of petty treason which involved the murder of a husband by a wife or a master by a servant. The privilege of sanctuary and the claim of benefit of clergy [an ancient exemption that had degenerated into allowing people who could read a few words to be tried by the usually more lenient Church courts] did not apply in cases of witchcraft. Tortures that were common elsewhere in Europe such as thumbscrews, strappado [tying a prisoner's hands behind his back and raising him off the floor], flogging, burning, tearing the flesh with hot irons and the bone-crushing 'boot' of Scotland, were not used in England because they were unlawful in such cases. Where 'torture' did occur it usually involved the deprivation of food and sleep to cause a suspect to become confused by exhaustion.

Some scandalous cases of fraud resulting in innocent people being executed on the evidence of supposedly bewitched children undermined James's belief in witchery to such an extent that the number of witch trials and executions declined dramatically during the later years of his reign. When James died in 1625 aged 58 he was buried in the grandeur of Westminster Abbey, but his witch laws did not die with him. They remained on the statute book for another hundred years to the terror of many old women and the profit of England's most infamous witchfinder.

In a quiet corner of rural Suffolk some 14 miles to the north-east of Bury St. Edmunds stands an isolated village church not far from Moneypot Hill, Gallows Hill and Magpie Green. It is the church of St Mary at Redgrave and inside is a large and imposing monument to Lord Chief Justice Sir John Holt who died in 1710. It shows him splendidly attired in wig and robes, and the Latin epitaph praises him as 'the watchful upholder, the keen defender, the brave guardian of the liberty and the laws of England.'

After wild days at university in Oxford, John Holt became a judge renowned for his integrity, fairness and good sense, and although it made him unpopular with the populace, time after time he directed juries to acquit supposed witches. It was a stand that was remarkably influential in bringing witch persecutions in Britain to an end.

But before John Holt made his home in Suffolk, the county had been the scene of several notorious witch trials. In 1645 there had been the mass execution of eighteen supposed witches, one of them an old village parson, all the result of the activities of the self-appointed witch-hunter Matthew Hopkins who is the main subject of this book. And in 1662 two widows from Lowestoft had been condemned in a landmark trial presided over by Lord Chief Justice Sir Matthew Hale, a judge who had not the slightest doubt about their guilt or the reality of witchcraft.

During that trial the court heard tales of children being bewitched; of a yeoman's cart being spelled so that it got stuck between gateposts; and of witchcraft causing a new chimney to collapse. A farmer whose pigs 'would leap and caper and immediately fall down and die' also complained of being 'taken with a lameness in his limbs and very much vexed with a great number of lice of an extraordinary bigness'. He said that he could not get rid of the lice no matter how many times he changed his shirts. And when an imp in the shape of a toad was held in a fire it vanished in a flash like exploding gunpowder. Such was the prominence of the trial that thirty years later it would be used as a model for the notorious Salem witch-hunt in America.

Although there was plenty of evidence of fraud, Judge Hale made his position clear and a report of the trial noted his damning remarks. 'That there were such creatures as witches he made no doubt at all, for first the scriptures had affirmed so much. Secondly, the wisdom of all nations had provided laws against such persons, which is an argument of their confidence of such a crime. And such has been the judgement of this kingdom, as appears by that Act of Parliament [King James's statute of 1604] which has provided punishments proportionable to the quality of the offence. And [he] desired them [the jury] strictly to observe their evidence; and desired the great God of Heaven to direct their hearts in this weighty thing they had in hand; for to condemn the innocent, and to let the guilty go free, are both an abomination to the Lord.'

Thirty-two years later, in 1694, Sir John Holt presided over another witch trial in Bury St Edmunds and his attitude was very different to that of his illustrious predecessor. Mother Munnings was said to have kept imps and caused the death of her landlord. A witness said he had seen her take two imps out of a basket. Judge Holt pointed out that the man had been on his way home from an ale house at the time and the 'imps' were probably nothing more than balls of wool she was going to spin. Mother Munnings was acquitted.

Sir John Holt was a man in tune with the new spirit of the late 17th century. Religious fanaticism was out of fashion after the traumas of the English Civil War, and opposition to belief in witches and witchcraft was growing fast among intellectuals. Scholarly opinion was swinging to the view that witchery was just another superstition, and although books urging its reality continued to be published, mockery, incredulity and the slow rise of science were taking their toll.

One of the most influential of late 17th century books supporting the belief in witchcraft was by Oxford educated theologian Joseph Glanvill, sometime chaplain to King Charles II and rector of the Abbey Church at Bath. His book *Sadducismus Triumphatus* appeared in 1681, a year after his death, and it was a much-enlarged version of an earlier work. In it he complained that those who denied the existence of spirits and witches were nothing less than atheists. 'Those that dare not bluntly say there is no God,' he wrote, 'content themselves to deny that there are spirits or witches.' But the tide of educated opinion was running against Glanvill and others like him, so much so that Glanvill had to admit that tales of witchery were things to be laughed at among the ruling class. Stories that once would have had men shaking in their shoes were being scorned as silly fireside tales and old wives' fables.

The knockout blow came in 1718 with the appearance of a book by another senior cleric, Francis Hutchinson, chaplain to King George I and later Bishop of Down. Significantly Hutchinson had had a long association with Bury St Edmunds and his interest in tales of witches had been aroused when he had been appointed vicar of St James's Church in that town. [St James's is now designated a cathedral.]

His book, *An Historical Essay concerning Witchcraft,* scorned the 'vulgar errors' of the superstition and, just as the witch-hunters quoted the Bible in support of their activities, so Hutchinson turned texts from the Old and New Testaments against the 'superstitious vanities' and 'old wives' fables.' The book and its many foreign translations attacked the folly of believing the imaginings of 'wicked persons and crack-brained girls' and it had the effect of virtually destroying any lingering belief in witchcraft among the educated ruling class. In 1736, three years before Hutchinson's death, King James's witchcraft laws were abolished. In England some 50 years had passed since the last hanging of a witch and it was nine years since the last burning in Scotland. Across Europe thousands of innocent men, women and children had been tortured and done to death in the name of a cruel delusion.

But in the story of English witchcraft one name looms larger in the popular imagination than that of any theologian, lawyer or king, and that name belongs to Matthew Hopkins, the self-styled Witchfinder General. He led the witch-hunt that was responsible for the execution of more people as witches in England than any other during the 170 years or so that the mania waxed and waned.

During the 1620s and 1630s, the years of Hopkins' youth, the number of witch trials had declined rapidly. Where once they had been regular and common events at county assizes, years went by without anyone coming before a judge and jury on a charge of witchery, and when they did the chance of conviction was small indeed. After the notorious cases of fraud by supposedly bewitched children at Leicester and Pendle earlier in the century, it seemed that the paranoia was dying away.

Then, in 1642, came civil war. Passions were inflamed by political animosities and religious bigotry. Families and communities were split by their allegiance to either King or Parliament, and after three years of increasingly bitter and brutal war, Matthew Hopkins took the first steps in his career as a witch-hunter.

He said his motive for hunting the Devil's 'delicate firebrand darlings' was neither money nor fame. He declared that he did it 'for the benefit of the whole kingdom', and denied that he had any special knowledge about how to conduct a witch-hunt. But the truth was that he did make money out of it; he did claim to have a special home-grown skill for smelling out witches, and, as his witch-hunt developed, he revelled in the fact that his name inspired fear and dread.

Hopkins' first victim was Elizabeth Clarke from Manningtree, an old one-legged beggar-woman without a tooth in her head. Hopkins and his friends bullied a confession out of her and soon she stood accused of bewitching to death a son of one of Hopkins' neighbours. She was also charged with keeping four imps – one like a white kitten, one like a fat spaniel without legs, another called Vinegar Tom 'like a long legged greyhound with an head like an ox' which could turn itself into a headless child, and one called Sack and Sugar which had the appearance of a black rabbit. Elizabeth Clarke was one of more than thirty women who were tried at Chelmsford assizes in July 1645. Most of them were from Tendring Hundred, an area in the north-east corner of Essex fringed by the North Sea and the rivers Stour and Colne. Four of the women were from Manningtree, four from Ramsey, five from St Osyth and others came from Great Clacton, Langham, Lawford, Wivenhoe and Thorpe-le-Soken.

Nineteen of the women rounded up by Hopkins and his friends were hanged, four more died in jail before coming to trial and 12 others were either held in jail or died there as a result of the terrible prison conditions of those days – the jargon of the times was 'by visitation of God'.

Hopkins' career as a witch-finder had begun.

The Contrivers of Men's Calamities

O*ne* Sunday in August 1577 a terrifying thunderstorm burst over the beautiful riverside church at Blythburgh in Suffolk. A bolt of lightning struck the tower and tons of stonework crashed through the roof. But the dazed men and women in the congregation did not blame the violent weather for the calamity. They declared that it was all the Devil's doing because they had seen with their own eyes a fiery demon burst through the door and strike a man and a boy 'stark dead'.

Then the summer storm had moved on and another thunderbolt struck a church a few miles away at Bungay. There people said the Devil had appeared in the shape of a monstrous black dog which killed two men, the 'monster' having 'wrung the necks of them both at one instant clean backward.'

When some of John Bird's pigs died in the Essex village of White Roding in 1565 people said they had been bewitched by widow Anne Vale. At Maidstone in Kent they blamed widow Joan Byden when some children fell ill and a few turkey cocks died. A year later William Higham of Hatfield Peverel blamed Laura Winchester for the death of his cows, sheep and pigs. She was declared innocent but old Agnes Waterhouse was not so lucky. She was accused of bewitching a neighbour to death, found guilty and hanged.

Events like these show how strong was the belief in the malice of the Devil and his legions of witches and demons.

Indeed, in the 16th century it was a belief shared by people of all classes thanks to years of preaching by men of the Church. Religious faith was strong but there was no science to explain why infants died suddenly, why the bodies of strong men wasted away, why beasts became diseased and why sometimes the cheese would not set and the beer would not brew.

Fate, destiny, accident, chance, call it what you will, but to the people of those days most things were explained as being the will of God or the work of the Devil. To people who believed that they shared their world with ghosts, fairies, evil spirits and lawless demons, witchcraft was an ever-present reality. It explained the blasts, blights, storms, strokes and other apparently causeless and random accidents and misfortunes that punctuated their hard and precarious lives.

In a world in which life for most men and women was lightened by few luxuries or comforts, the concept of witchcraft was neither absurd nor illogical. Why should ordinary people think the notion of turkey cocks being bewitched was ridiculous when educated men asserted that witches could fly through the air on broomsticks if they rubbed their bodies with an ointment made from the boiled bones of children, and that those flying witches could be brought down by ringing the church bells?

Why should they disbelieve tales of witches collecting men's penises when those tales were recorded by high officials of the Inquisition? According to one such story, a man who asked a witch to restore his missing organ was told to choose one from the dozens stored in a bird's nest high in the branches of a tree. Eagerly he climbed up and picked out a big one only to be told to put it back because it belonged to the parish priest! Could such a story be considered ridiculous when learned scholars declared that a female demon called a succubus [from the Latin for whore] could take semen from a sleeping man or a male corpse, change shape into a male demon [incubus] and then copulate with and impregnate a sleeping woman?

In 1608 Bishop Joseph Hall showed how deeply ingrained superstitions were when he wrote almost despairingly about the gullibility of many of his fellows. 'In the morning he listens whether the crow cries even or odd and by that token presages of the weather. If he hear but a raven croak from the next roof or if a bittern flies over his head by night he makes his will. If his troubled fancy shall second his thoughts with the dream of a fair garden or green rushes or the salutation of a dead friend he takes leave of the world and says he cannot live. Old wives and stars are his counsellors: his nightspell is his guard; and charms his physicians. He wears Paracelsian characters for the toothache and a little hallowed wax is his antidote for all evils. Some ways he will not go and some he dares not; either there are bugs [hobgoblins], or he feigns them. Every lantern is a ghost and every noise is of chains.' [Paracelsus was a Swiss alchemist, physician and philosopher who had some odd ideas about medical treatment and was said to keep an imp in the pommel of his sword.]

A century later Daniel Defoe described the English as 'addicted to prophecies, astrological conjurations, dreams and old wives' tales' and that gullibility endures judging by the modern appetite for horoscopes, crystals and plastic pyramids.

As witch-mania tightened its grip in the 16th and 17th centuries, religious disputes, war and bigotry inflamed the climate of superstition. Demonologists, particularly French and German ones, wrote about hierarchies of demons and devils, and pronounced on how to detect witches and how to counteract their spells.

In 1590 London lawyer William West wrote a guide to English law in which he described a witch as someone who was deluded by the Devil into believing she could do all sorts of evil deeds such as 'to shake the air with lightning and thunder, cause hail and tempests, remove green corn or trees to another place, to be carried by her familiar which has taken upon him the deceitful shape of a goat, swine, calf, etc. into some mountain far distant, in a wonderful space of time. And sometimes to fly upon a staff or fork, or some other instrument and to spend all the night after with her sweetheart in playing, sporting, banqueting, dalliance and divers other devilish lusts and lewd disports.'

Other kinds of witches were, he said, diviners who used spirits to find lost or stolen goods; those who thought they could enchant or charm using words, herbs or images; jugglers who cured sickness with charms hung around the necks of men or beasts; magicians who 'falsely pretended' to summon ghosts by magic words; and soothsayers and wizards who told the future by gazing into glasses or crystal balls.

Reginald Scot, an early critic of English witch-hunting whose book *The Discovery of Witchcraft* was ordered to be burned by King James, tried to counter such ideas by saying that there were but four types of witches – the innocent who were falsely accused; the self-deluded and the crazed; poisoners; and fraudulent healers and fortune-tellers. And none of them, he said, could do anything by supernatural means. Scot was a country squire from Kent who had been horrified by the injustices done 'to old women here on earth' in the witch-hunts that had followed the re-introduction of witchcraft laws by Queen Elizabeth I in 1563.

'The fables of witchcraft have taken so fast hold and deep root in the hearts of men,' he wrote, 'that few or none can nowadays with patience endure the hand and correction of God. For if any adversity, grief, sickness, loss of children, corn, cattle, or liberty happen unto them; by and by they exclaim upon witches. As though there were no God in Israel that orders all things according to his will; punishing both just and unjust with griefs, plagues and afflictions in manner and form as he thinks good; but that certain old women here on earth called witches, must needs be the contrivers of all men's calamities and as though they themselves were innocents and had deserved no such punishments.'

Although people feared witchcraft, the popularity and reputation of the white or blessing witches remained high. Indeed, as Scot affirmed, it was to the cunning man or wise woman that people went in search of 'comfort and remedy in time of their tribulation.' To the great mass of ordinary people the curing witch was a wizard or magician in the sense of a sage and healer. They were valued members of the community whose knowledge and skills gave them a role combining those of physician, chemist and counsellor. So high were their reputations that many people thought the wise woman or the cunning man more effective than any doctor with his potion or any priest with his prayers.

But to many clerics and preachers the white witch was as bad as any black or hurting witch. 'Sorcerers are too common; cunning men, wizards and white witches, as they call them, are in every village, which if they be sought unto, will help almost all infirmities of body and mind,' said Oxford theologian Robert Burton. 'It is a common practice of some men to go first to a witch and then to a physician; if one cannot [cure] the other shall.' Another churchman complained that 'common ignorants are besotted with the opinion of their skill,' and the uncompromising Calvinist William Perkins who preached in Cambridge and who, until his death in 1602, was considered England's greatest witchcraft expert, acknowledged that 'charmers are more sought unto than physicians in time of need.'

Doctors did not enjoy the best of reputations. 'An unlearned and so unworthy physician is a kind of horseleech whose cure is most in drawing of blood and a desperate purge, either to cure or kill, as it hits,' said the poet Nicholas Breton in 1616 in a description that would fit a quack doctor of any age. 'He is never without merry tales and stale jests to make old folk laugh, and comfits [sugared dried fruit] or plums in his pocket to please little children; yea, and he will be talking of complexions though he know nothing of their dispositions; and if his medicine do a feat, he is a made man among fools; but being wholly unlearned and oftimes unhonest, let me thus briefly describe him: he is a plain kind of mountebank and a true quacksalver, a danger for the sick to deal with, and a dizard [prattling fool] in the world to talk with.'

'Many deny witches at all, or, if there be any, they can do no harm, but on the contrary are most lawyers, divines, physicians, philosophers,' wrote clergyman Robert Burton in 1621. The opposition of doctors was a result of their own ignorance because, as the sceptic Thomas Ady later explained, 'Seldom goes any man or woman to a physician for cure of any disease but one question they ask the physician is, 'Sir, do you not think this party is in an ill handling, or under an ill tongue?' or, more plainly, 'Sir, do you not think the party is bewitched?' and to this many an ignorant physician will answer, 'Yes, verily'. When he cannot find the nature of the disease, he says the party is bewitched.'

Since the days before the Norman Conquest it had been believed that kings had the healing touch for morbus regius which at first meant leprosy and later scrofula and other unsightly maladies of the face and neck. So popular was the belief that people would journey to London to be 'touched' by the sovereign. Although they considered it superstitious, Queen Elizabeth I and King James I participated in the ritual, and King Charles II enjoyed bestowing the royal touch so much that over the years he administered it to 100,000 people.

A charm of the times 'to heal the King's or Queen's evil or any soreness in the throat was first to touch the place with the hand of one that died an untimely death, otherwise let a virgin fasting lay her hand on the sore and say, Apollo denies that the heat of the plague can increase where a naked virgin quenches it, and spit three times upon it.'

It prompted some cynics to ask what was it that distinguished a king from a village charmer? Despite the opposition of doctors who disliked the competition, and condemnation by theologians who said they were dealers with the Devil, the village wizards were kept busy. In 1807, some two-hundred years after the days of Perkins, Burton and Breton, their skills were still profitable as the poet Robert Southey reported, 'A cunning man or a cunning woman, as they are termed, is to be found near every town, and though the laws are occasionally put in force against them, still it is a gainful trade.'

The roots of the belief in witchcraft were deep and strong among the 'common ignorants' of Tudor and Stuart England. To them witchery was a two-edged sword. There was black magic and white magic. The witch or hag might blight their crops, injure their animals or bewitch their households, but the wise woman and the cunning man knew when it was a good time to go on a journey or to get married, and might even concoct a love potion. They could read your fortune in the stars or in the lines on your hands, offer healing tonics when you were sick, and they knew what to do when you, your wife, your child, your cows or your pigs were bewitched.

But Puritan preacher William Perkins saw things very differently. To him a witch was a witch, black or white. 'According to the vulgar conceit,' he said, 'distinction is usually made betwixt the white and the black witch; the good and the bad witch. The bad witch they are wont to call him or her that works malefice or mischiefs to the bodies of men and beasts; the good witch they count him or her that helps to reveal, prevent or remove the same.' In his *Discourse of the Damned*

Art of Witchcraft he went on, 'Though the witch were in many respects profitable, and did not hurt, but procured much good, yet because he has renounced God, his king and governor, and has bound himself by other laws to the service of the enemies of God and his Church, death is his portion justly assigned him by God; he may not live... it were a thousand times better for the land if all witches, but specially the blessing witch might suffer death. Death is the just and deserved portion of the good witch.'

Hopkins' witch-hunting partner John Stearne agreed. He declared, 'But yet I say all witches be bad, and ought to suffer alike, being both in league with the Devil: for so is the good, so untruly called, as well as the other, either open or implicit. And therefore I conclude, all that be in open league with the Devil ought to die.'

The word witch comes from the Old English words wicca meaning a male witch and wicce, a female witch. They were supposed to have the power to wiccian – to bewitch or work sorcery. Over time witch came to mean much the same as sorcerer although originally a sorcerer was someone who practised divination, that is the attempted prediction of events or the revealing of secrets by supernatural means. The belief that sorcery was evil came from the idea that sorcerers raised demons or spirits. Revealing the future by pretended communication with the dead was termed necromancy from the Greek nekros, corpse, and manteia, divination.

Writers about witchcraft listed many curious methods of divination. Alectyromancy was foretelling the future by interpreting the way chickens pecked at grain; chiromancy was the study of hands [now it is usually called palmistry]; cleromancy used dice; coscinomancy used sieve and shears and it was also a popular method of detecting thieves; gastromancy involved listening to the sounds coming from a person's stomach; gyromancy was walking in a circle until dizzy and predicting the future by the way you fell over; oneiromancy was the interpretation of dreams; scatomancy was divination by looking at dung; and tyromancy involved watching cheese set.

Words such as magician, conjuror, juggler and enchanter were used to describe different types of witches. Cunning, which meant learning and wisdom, and words such as wile, guile and crafty meaning to have skill, came to imply deception. Beguile meant to delude by trickery. A charm could be an incantation as well as an amulet or talisman such as a rabbit's foot carried for good luck. So to charm as far as witches were supposed to have the power to charm meant to subdue, summon, or have power over others by means of occult influence. Spell once meant a tale or story and came to mean a verse or phrase that acquired magical or protective power when repeated. 'His nightspell is his guard,' Bishop Joseph Hall had said of superstitious men, and a popular nightspell in the 17th century was the rhyme –

Matthew, Mark, Luke and John, the bed be blest that I lie on,
Four angels to my bed. Four angels round my head.
One to watch, and one to pray, and two to bear my soul away.

Other words meaning much the same as bewitched and charmed, that is to be the target of or subject to a witch's powers, included spellbound, enchanted, forspoken and, if done by the evil eye, overlooked and fascinated. Bewitched animals were sometimes described as fairy-taken, elf-shot or owl-blasted. The words wizard and magician originally had nothing to do with sorcery, and witch and witchcraft do not come from linguistic roots meaning knowledge or wisdom.

Witchcraft was not a lost or suppressed pagan fertility religion, nor was it a craft or art secretly preserved from ancient times in the face of persecution by the Christian Church. It was an invented heresy forged within specifically European social and religious circumstances under the impact of a fusion of satanophobia, arcane superstitions, and a mish-mash of obsolete customs, archaic traditions and folklore.

The defining point about witchcraft as far as the Christian Church was concerned was the idea that the witch was a Devil-worshipper and an apostate. Witches were the new heretics. They were soldiers in the army of the antichrist, and witch-hunters justified their actions by quoting Bible texts such as Exodus 22.18 'Thou shalt not suffer a witch to live' and Deuteronomy 18.10-12 'There shall not be found among you any one that maketh his son or his daughter to pass through the fire, or that useth divination, or an observer of times [dreams], or an enchanter, or a witch. Or a charmer, or a consulter with familiar spirits, or a wizard, or a necromancer. For all that do these things are an abomination unto the Lord: and because of these abominations the Lord thy God doth drive them out from before thee.' Christian fundamentalists of more recent years have used Bible texts to condemn other supposed Devil-inspired 'abominations' such as rock 'n' roll music, plays, films and TV programmes. Even the phenomenally successful 'Harry Potter' stories have attracted their wrath.

But the witch as understood by King James and his superstitious subjects was based on mistranslation and error. Critics of witch-mania pointed out that the Old Testament witch was not a Devil-worshipper at all but usually a fortune-teller of one sort or another, and all of them were frauds and tricksters. The best-known Old Testament witch is the Witch of Endor who was consulted by King Saul before a battle with the Philistines. She raised the ghost of Saul's predecessor, Samuel, who delivered a most discouraging prediction. The Witch of Endor was not a witch in the sense that King James, Judge Holt or Matthew Hopkins understood the term. She was a fortune-teller with a good line in ventriloquism and an accomplice in a white sheet.

As Christianity became the dominant religion across Europe so the Church took the view that witchcraft was fantasy. Witches flying at night, changing into animals and having the power to bewitch were all declared to be illusions sent by Satan. The gods of the ancient world, Egypt, Greece, Rome, as well as the gods of the Vikings and other heathens, were declared to be idols worshipped by people who had been tricked by the Devil. For decades it was Church policy to say that witchcraft was no more than the delusion of 'wicked women' who had fallen into 'pagan error'. But as the centuries passed the character of the Devil [Satan] was changed within Christianity. Satan the accuser; Satan the tester of religious faith as in the case of Job who was afflicted with boils from head to toe; Satan the adversary of Man, became Satan the enemy of God and Satan the 'great dragon.... that old serpent' of Revelations who had been cast out of Heaven with his host of fallen angels.

So the idea grew that the world was infested with millions of demons intent on overthrowing the Church of Christ, and witches were part of the hellish Devil-inspired plot. The reasoning was that witches received their powers from or perpetrated their wicked deeds through the agency of spirits. Those spirits were evil so, by definition, they must have come from the Devil, and therefore witches were in league with Satan. In short, witches had to die because they were heretics who had turned their backs on the promise of salvation. Some critics said that the malicious acts attributed to witches were often accidents which would have happened anyway and that the ever-deceitful Devil merely deluded witches into thinking they had the power to cause injury, death or disaster.

It was the Inquisition, the Church's thought police, who invented this doctrine of heretical witchcraft, and late in the 15th century it was given a new impetus by two events which at first had little influence in Britain. Heinrich Kramer and Jakob Sprenger were two senior officials in the Inquisition who complained that their witch-hunts in Germany were being hindered by local officials who denied that any witchery was going on. So Kramer and Sprenger appealed to Pope Innocent VIII and in 1484 he issued a Bull stating that he knew very well that witches were doing all sorts of wicked things like dealing with devils, destroying crops and animals, and stopping husbands and wives making love. He ordered the inquisitors to root out 'the abominations and enormities' of witchcraft as they saw fit and no one, whatever his rank, station or condition, was to question their authority on pain of excommunication or 'other more terrible punishments'.

Armed with this backing from Rome, Kramer and Sprenger set about their work and two years later they published their infamous book *Malleus Maleficarum* [The Hammer against Witches]. Because it had the pope's approval its influence was immediate and enormous, particularly in France and Germany, and it was re-issued again and again in various languages during the next hundred years. Witches, said Kramer and Sprenger, were heretics who served the Devil by sacrificing unbaptised children, engaging in orgies, making men's penises invisible, raising storms and so on. According to them it was heretical to even doubt the existence of witches. Their book was an encyclopaedia of witchcraft and it became the Church's approved handbook for witch-hunters. Full of fantasy, fable and perverted logic, it laid down the methods to be used to obtain confessions, including the use of torture and making false promises of mercy.

It expounded a venomously anti-feminine message by declaring that women were more likely to be witches because the Devil specifically targeted that sex. They said women were gossips, vain and impulsive liars with the brains of children, and that they were more sensual and carnal than men. A woman was 'an imperfect animal' because she had been formed from a rib 'which is bent in the contrary direction to a man'. In short they were a necessary evil. John Knox who led Scotland's religious revolution, described women as 'weak, frail, unpatient, feeble and foolish', and John Stearne, Hopkins' witch-hunting partner, said women had a more credulous nature, were apt to be misled, were commonly impatient and when displeased they were more malicious and that made them 'fit instruments for the Devil'.

Because witchcraft was an exceptional crime and difficult to prove in the normal way, and because, as Sprenger and Kramer said, the most damning evidence was a witch's own confession, torture was to be used as a matter of course. Judicial torture of the cruellest kind was inflicted on suspected witches almost everywhere except in England. In France, Italy, Germany and Scotland the accused was treated barbarously until they confessed, and the torture usually continued until the victim named more witches. If the confession were retracted the victim would be tortured again. Other writers exaggerated and enlarged on Kramer and Sprenger's ridiculous tales and wicked ideas. Even King James recycled some of them in his own book in which he estimated the ratio of female to male witches at twenty to one.

Another 'expert' thought it was more likely to be a hundred to one. A common idea about witches was that they kept imps or familiars, and Hopkins was to make great play of it in the evidence he brought against his victims. Other common ideas were that each and every witch had the Devil's mark and a witch's mark somewhere on his or her body. The witch's mark could be a wart or pimple and it was supposed to be the spot at which the imp was suckled. The Devil's mark was a spot, blemish or area of discoloured skin like a birthmark, and because it was the Devil's own brand mark it was supposed to be insensitive to pain. Thomas Ady answered such assertions by pointing out that Old Testament witches were more often men than women, and, he asked, 'Where is it written in all the old and new testaments that a witch is a murderer or has the power to kill by witchcraft, or to afflict with any disease or infirmity? Where is it written that witches have imps suckling of their bodies? Where is it written that witches have biggs [nipples] for imps to suck.....that the devil sets privy marks upon witches.... that witches can hurt corn or cattle or can fly in the air? Where do we read of a he-devil or a she-devil called incubus or succubus that uses generation or copulation?' In England and Scotland many of those indicted for witchcraft were pauper women and quarrelsome old widows. In 1645 all the thirty or more witches tried at Chelmsford as a result of Hopkins' first witch-hunt were women. At Bury St Edmunds in the summer of that year only a dozen of the one hundred witches held in jail were men.

Samuel Harsnett, who was born in Colchester in 1561 and later became Archbishop of York, was a thorough sceptic as far as witchcraft was concerned yet the picture he painted of the typical witch remains the popular stereotype today. He described a witch as 'an old weather-beaten crone, having the chin and her knees meeting of age, walking like a bow, leaning on a staff, hollow eyed, untoothed, furrowed on her face, having her limbs trembling with the palsy, going mumbling in the streets; one that has forgotten her paternoster [Lord's Prayer] and yet has a shrewd [sharp] tongue to call a drab a drab.' Drab meant slut or harlot.

The Rev. John Gaule, an opponent of Hopkins' witch-hunting,

described how easy it was for an old woman to be branded a witch. 'Every old woman with a wrinkled face, a furrowed brow, a hairy lip, a gobber tooth, a squint eye, a squeaking voice, or a scolding tongue, having a rugged coat on her back, a skullcap on her head, a spindle in her hand, and a dog or cat by her side, is not only suspected but pronounced for a witch.' Others writers described witches as 'miserable wretches so odious to all their neighbours', 'the basest sort of people' and 'poor and peevish old creatures'.

Half a century later Joseph Addison noted, 'When an old woman begins to dote and grow chargeable to a parish, she is generally turned into a witch and fills the whole community with extravagant fancies, imaginary distempers and terrifying dreams. In the meantime, the poor wretch that is the innocent occasion of so many evils, begins to be frighted at herself and sometimes confesses secret commerces and familiarities that her imagination forms in a delirious old age. This frequently cuts off charity from the greatest objects of compassion, and inspires people with a malevolence towards those poor decrepit parts of our species, in whom human nature is defaced by infirmity and dotage.'

Thomas Ady noted that it was often claimed that strange things began to happen after a beggar-woman had been sent away empty-handed. It prompted him to write, 'If a man suffers in his estate or health, presently he cries out of some poor innocent neighbour that he or she has bewitched him; for, says he, such an old man or woman was lately at my door and desired some relief and I denied it, and, God forgive me, my heart did rise against her at that time, my mind gave me she looked like a witch, and presently my child, my wife, my self, my horse, my cow, my sheep, my sow, my hog, my dog, my cat or somewhat was thus and thus handled, in such a strange manner, as I dare swear she is a witch, or else how should these things be or come to pass?'

In recent years some historians have endeavoured to depict the European witch-mania as a 'gender war', a conspiracy devised by priests and judges - all of them male - to intimidate and suppress any movement toward independence by sexually active women. While it is true that more women than men suffered in the English witch-hunts, the persecutions were always more anti-witch that anti-female. In Europe the numbers of male and female witches that were accused varied at different times and in different places. The reason why there were witch-hunts at all was because, in most cases, people genuinely believed that witches existed and that their lives were being blighted by their witchcraft.

Almost all the witches tried in Britain were prosecuted under laws that were in force from 1563 to 1736. There had been laws against sorcery before then, even back in the times of the Anglo-Saxon kings, but it was in 1542, in the closing years of the reign of King Henry VIII, that Parliament passed an Act against 'invocation or conjurations of spirits, witchcrafts, enchantments or sorceries'. Until then sorcery usually meant things like providing protective charms, concocting love potions, fortune-telling, and 'fantastical practices' to discover buried treasure or recover stolen goods. These had been dealt with by Church courts and the usual punishment was some form of penance.

As well as making it a felony to use witchcraft to destroy or harm people or property, 'to provoke any person to unlawful love', or 'to tell or declare where goods stolen or lost shall become', the Act of 1542 made witchcraft a crime 'for any unlawful intent or purpose'. The punishment decreed was death along with the forfeiture of land and property. It seems that this statute was never invoked and it was repealed in 1547, the first year of the reign of the boy-king Edward VI. England was then ruled by that young king's uncle, Edward Seymour, Duke of Somerset, as Lord Protector of the Realm. It was said that when the astrologer Robert Allen cast a horoscope predicting the young king's death, Somerset had Allen and his paraphernalia of the 'devilish arts' dragged before the council. Allen protested that the repeal of the 1542 statute by Somerset himself had made his craft lawful. 'You foolish knave,' retorted Somerset who had no time for superstition and idolatry. 'If you and all that be of your science tell me what I shall do tomorrow, I will give you all that I have,' he barked and sent the Norfolk 'wizard and bawd' to cool his heels in the Tower of London.

But when Queen Elizabeth I came to the throne there was a growing mood that England needed laws against witchcraft and so a new statute was enacted in 1563. Anti-witchcraft legislation also came into force in Scotland that year. The English laws were extended to Ireland in 1586. The preamble to Queen Elizabeth's statute stated that since the repeal of her father's witch laws 'many devilish persons have devised and practised invocations and conjurations of evil and wicked spirits, and have used and practised witchcrafts, enchantments, charms and sorceries to the destruction of the persons and goods of their neighbours and other subjects of this realm, and for other lewd intents and purposes contrary to the laws of Almighty God, to the peril of their own souls and to the great infamy and disquietness of this realm.'

The 1563 Act was the result of increasing pressure from the new Protestant preaching clerics, many of whom were imbued with radical ideas gained during exile when Elizabeth's Roman Catholic half-sister Mary had been queen. There was also the desire of Elizabeth's ministers to establish a stable regime in those turbulent times. [The Tudors were always conscious of their flimsy claim to the throne. On the male side, Henry VII's grandfather had been an obscure squire, one Owen Tudor from Anglesey, who had seduced and secretly married the widow of England's hero-king, Henry V. On his mother's side, Henry VII's claim came from a bastard son, later legitimated, born to John of Gaunt and his mistress.] As well as the witch laws, Parliament re-introduced laws against spreading 'fantastic prophecies' which might lead to political unrest and in 1581 it was made a felony to cast the Queen's horoscope in an effort to predict how long she might live and who would succeed her.

It was no threat to the government if a few sheep or pigs were 'bewitched', but laws which dealt with such things could easily be used against trouble-mongering astrologers, fortune-tellers, 'prophets' or ambitious aristocrats who trespassed into any area that smacked of treason. Although the 1563 statute was less rigorous than that of Henry VIII, it was regularly invoked and scores of witches were tried

A
CONFIRMATION
And Difcovery of
WITCH CRAFT,

Containing thefe feverall particulars;

That there are Witches called
bad Witches, and Witches untruely called
good or white Witches, and what manner of
people they be, and how they may bee knowne,
with many particulars thereunto tending.

Together with the Confeffions of many of thofe executed fince
May 1645. in the feverall Counties hereafter mentioned.
As alfo fome objeftions Anfwered.

By *John Stearne,* now of *Lawfhall* neere *Burie*
Saint *Edmonds* in *Suffolke,* fometimes of
Manningtree in *Effex.*

PROV.17.15. *He that juftifieth the wicked, and he that condemneth the juft, even they
both are an abomination to the Lord.*
DEVT 13.14. *Thou fhalt therefore inquire, and make fearch, and afke diligently,
whether it be truth, and the thing certaine.*

LONDON,
Printed by *William Wilfon,* dwelling in Little Saint *Bartholo-
mewes* neere *Smithfield.* 1 6 4 8

*The cover of the book published in 1648 by Hopkin's witch-hunting
partner, John Stearne. It gives his version of many of the events that
occurred during their infamous witch-hunt across East Anglia.*

and executed during Elizabeth's reign. The statute retained the death sentence for invoking evil spirits or killing by witchcraft. Causing injury to people or the destruction of property or livestock was to be punished by death at the second offence. Divination for treasure or lost or stolen goods, provoking unlawful love, or intending to kill or harm by witchery were to be punished by a year in jail with four terms in the pillory for the first offence, and life imprisonment on a second conviction with perhaps the forfeiture of property.

The pillory punishment involved the felon standing with his or her head and wrists clamped in a wooden frame for six hours in a town market place where the offender was to 'openly confess his or her error and offence.' The purpose of the pillory, which was the usual punishment for dishonest traders, drunks, scolds and whores, was that the offender should also suffer public ridicule and humiliation as well as the peril of having stones and dung thrown at her by the populace. Its use was abolished in 1837. And as before and later, those charged with witchcraft were not allowed to claim the privilege of sanctuary or benefit of clergy, an ancient exemption that ended in 1827.

On March 24, 1603, Elizabeth I died at Richmond Palace and the Tudor dynasty died with her. A year later King James's more rigorous laws 'for the better restraining and more severe punishing' of acts of 'conjuration, witchcraft and dealing with evil and wicked spirits' came into effect. It was the new king's opinion that English witches convicted of killing were put to death more for being murderers than for being witches. Where Elizabeth's law had made life imprisonment the penalty, James made it death, and death was to be the only penalty for acts 'whereby any person shall be killed, destroyed, wasted, consumed, pined or lamed in his or her body, or any part thereof' and for digging up 'any dead man, woman or child out of his, her, or their graves, or any other place where the dead body rests, or the skin, bone, or any other part of any dead person, to be employed or used in any manner of witchcraft, sorcery, charm or enchantment.' And as for imps or familiar spirits, James made it a felony to 'consult, covenant with, entertain, employ, feed, or reward any evil and wicked spirit to or for any intent or purpose'.

The number of prosecutions under King James's statute rose and fell during the early years of the 17th century and reached a peak in 1645-6 as a result of Hopkins' activities. The last execution for witchcraft in England was at Exeter in 1684 and Scotland's last one was in 1727. Nine years later the English witch laws of King James I and the Scottish witch laws of his mother, Mary Queen of Scots, were repealed. Parliament ordered that from June 24, 1736, 'no prosecution, suit or proceeding shall be commenced or carried on against any person or persons for witchcraft, sorcery, enchantment or conjuration, or for charging another with any such offence, in any court whatsoever in Great Britain.'

The statute went on to add that anyone pretending to exercise 'witchcraft, sorcery, enchantment or conjuration or undertake to tell fortunes, or pretend from his or her skill or knowledge in any occult or crafty science, to discover where or in what manner any goods or chattels, supposed to have been stolen or lost, may be found' would be prosecuted for actions 'whereby ignorant persons are frequently deluded and defrauded'. The punishment would be a year in jail, four appearances in the pillory and an obligation to give sureties for his or her good behaviour. It was the age of enlightenment and in the eyes of the law, wizards and witches were cheats and their supposed craft was a fraud.

A belief that had been an unquestioned element in the creed of kings and peasants was fast being reduced to fable and taradiddle. Times had changed and in law at least witchcraft had been relegated to the world of fantasy. Mockery, scepticism and revulsion at the cruel persecution of old women were part of the cause. Other reasons included new study of the scriptures which had led to the Devil and his demons being downgraded in mainstream Christian theology, and the view among intellectuals and judges that the whole matter rested on religious obscurantism, absurdities and impossibilities.

High Sorcery and Common Witchery

*T*he most famous magician in British mythology is Merlin, the legendary mentor of King Arthur. According to the 12th century monk and chronicler, Geoffrey of Monmouth, the Welsh wizard was conceived in a most unusual way. Merlin's mother was a woman of noble birth who became a nun and she was visited at night by a handsome young man who could make himself invisible. In other words Merlin's father was an incubus demon from the far side of the moon. Theologians said incubi were lecherous fallen angels which, unlike the demons that caused nightmares, enjoyed making love to women. [The modern versions of incubi are bug-eyed aliens from outer space which abduct members of the human race – usually Americans – in order to conduct bizarre sexual experiments in UFOs.]

For years there had been speculation about how a spirit-being such as an incubus could transform itself into a physical body in order to enjoy the sexual relations necessary to make a woman pregnant. One learned friar declared that the demons either re-animated corpses or made totally new bodies for themselves out of a mixture of unspecified materials. Another demonologist said the story of Merlin's conception was wrong and he had been as human as anyone else. What had happened was that the demon had enlarged the woman with wind and then given her a stolen child. Sceptics said the idea of sex-mad demons was rubbish and it was just a convenient excuse for any wife, widow or unmarried woman who had the misfortune to fall pregnant as a result of the attentions of her very real human lover, particularly if that lover happened to be a priest or monk.

The old chronicles tell many tales of sorcery and witchery. There is one about King Duff of Scotland who ruled 962-967. His doctors were baffled when he was sorely afflicted in his body by a strange sweating sickness and it seemed that he was doomed to die. Then came the news that three witches had been found roasting an image of him over a fire. They were burnt at Forres [a stone marks the spot] and Duff's health immediately improved. Shakespeare must have known the tale because in his 'Scottish play' he has Macbeth [reigned 1040-1057] encounter three 'secret, black and midnight hags....so wither'd and so wild in their attire' in a cavern near Forres. William of Malmesbury, another 12th century historian monk, told the tale of a woman from Berkeley who sold her soul to the Devil in return for a life of feasting and debauchery. One day her pet jackdaw started screeching and she realised that her end was near. Terrified, she confessed her dreadful secret to her children and pleaded with them to prevent the Devil taking her body. But all their efforts were in vain. Although her stone coffin was bound with chains and a choir of priests chanted psalms, a gang of demons smashed their way into the church, broke open the tomb and her screaming corpse was dragged off to Hell by the Devil on the back of a big black horse.

Rather more credible is the story of Dame Alice Kyteler of Kilkenny who was accused of sorcery and heresy. She had acquired great wealth from her four marriages but a bitter feud among her children over who should inherit resulted in a bishop bringing charges against her and her favourite son in 1324. It was said that Dame Alice had a demon lover called Robin and that she and her accomplices parodied Christian ceremonies and indulged in sexual orgies. Alice was accused of making foul concoctions in a skull and using them to kill her first three husbands and slowly poison the fourth. It was claimed that she sacrificed cocks and 'swept the streets of Kilkenny, raking all the filth toward the doors of her son, murmuring and muttering secretly with herself these words, To the house of William my son, hie all the wealth of Kilkenny town.' Although she had considerable influence in high places, the bishop won the long legal struggle and Dame Alice retreated to England leaving one of her maids to be burned.

Kings found sorcery a convenient charge to bring against over-mighty subjects and organisations. The Templars, an order of knights founded in 1118 to protect pilgrims in the Holy Land, was suppressed in 1312 amid charges of Satanism, heresy and orgies with succubi demons. The bankrupt King of France and England's Edward II were among those who profited from the order's confiscated wealth. A decade later twenty-seven burghers of Coventry who complained of high taxes were tried and acquitted of conspiring to kill the same King Edward, the Prior of Coventry and others by employing a magician to stick needles into wax models.

Alice Perrers, the avaricious mistress of Edward III, was accused of gaining royal favour by 'wicked enchantments', and political rivalry at the court of Henry VI led to a charge of treasonous sorcery being made against Eleanor, the second wife and former mistress of Humphrey, Duke of Gloucester. The duke was the king's uncle and, more importantly at the time, heir to the throne. With the aid of 'a cunning man in astronomy', a priest and Margery Jourdemain, the 'witch of Eye', Eleanor foolishly indulged in some sorcery and fortune-telling to see if she might be queen one day. Her accomplices were executed for treason with 'the witch of Eye' being burned. The duchess was declared guilty by a court of bishops, made to walk barefoot while carrying a candle through the streets of London as a public penance and was then exiled to the Isle of Man.

Jacquetta, the one time Duchess of Bedford and Eleanor's sister-in-law, was said to have used witchcraft to ensnare Edward IV into secretly marrying her widowed daughter, Elizabeth Woodville. According to her enemies the result was that England suffered 'many murders, extortions and oppressions' with 'every good maiden and woman standing in dread to be ravished and defouled.' Edward's brother Richard, Duke of York, used the old rumour to justify declaring Edward's children bastards and so open the way for his seizure of the throne as Richard III. He also accused Edward's queen, Elizabeth Woodville, and mistress, Elizabeth Shore, of using sorcery to wither his arm. In Scotland in 1479 James III accused one of his brothers of using sorcery against him and some 'witches and wizards' were burned at Edinburgh. Janet Douglas, Lady Glamis, suffered the same fate in 1537 for trying to kill the newly married James V by witchcraft.

In 1521 Edward Stafford, Duke of Buckingham, was executed for treason tainted with divination. He had consulted a crystal-gazing monk famed for his prophecies and had been told that he would be king if Henry VIII had no son. Elizabeth Barton 'the holy maid of Kent' gained a reputation as a prophetess and dared to tell Henry VIII that he would not live long if he married Anne Boleyn. Henry took the matter seriously for a time but when the prophecy had been proved false she was hanged at Tyburn. But when Anne failed to provide a male heir, Henry became convinced that their marriage was cursed and that sorcery had been used to seduce him into the union. These episodes involved the high and the mighty. The English witch-hunts that sent scores of commoners to the gallows followed the passing of new witch laws in 1562, a hundred years or more after witch-hunting had become firmly established in continental Europe. There the Inquisition had brought sorcery within the scope of its activities by making it a religious crime with the inquisitors empowered to use torture and seize a victim's goods. Witch-mania, an invention of theologians who transformed folklore and traditional sorcery into a satanic cult, allowed the Inquisition to create a new class of heretics. And while that helped to justify the organisation's existence, it also replenished their coffers with some of the spoils.

England's experience of witch-mania was shorter and much less cruel and bloody. This was because witchcraft was a civil crime; because tortures that were routinely used in other countries were not allowed; and because the wilder continental ideas such as sabbats, sexual orgies, flying on broomsticks, sacrificing babies and kissing the Devil's buttocks were discountenanced. The English were usually more concerned with the alleged murder, injury or damage done by a witch than by any supposed Satanism, and that was one of the reasons why James I changed the law in 1604.

The first known execution of a witch in England was in 1566 when widow Agnes Waterhouse from Hatfield Peverel was hanged for killing a man by her witchery. She admitted sending her imp, an old white spotted cat called Satan, to drown a neighbour's cow, kill geese and stop butter coming. She had been given the cat by Elizabeth Francis who was jailed for a year after she confessed to using the same cat to kill a man who had refused to marry her. She also admitted killing her own child and laming her quarrelsome husband. Twelve years later Elizabeth Francis would be hanged for bewitching a woman to death.

During the last quarter of the 16th century the number of witch trials increased, particularly in Essex, and the number of supposed witches appearing at the twice-yearly assizes rose from the usual one or two a time to five, six, seven or more. In 1582 thirteen women were rounded up in and around St Osyth in Tendring Hundred and charged with bewitching men, women, children, beasts, beer-brewings, milk and cream. The evidence followed a pattern that would become familiar. Witnesses told how mishaps began to occur after angry words were exchanged with the old women. Ursula Kemp, who eked out a living by child-minding and healing aches and pains with charms and incantations, said 'though she could unwitch she could not witch.' She was annoyed when a woman refused to let her nurse a new-born child which not long after fell out of its cradle and broke its neck. Then when the mother refused to pay Ursula the shilling fee for curing 'a lameness in her bones' the ailment returned. Evidence was also given against Ursula by her young bastard son. He said his mother had four imps – 'Titty is like a little grey cat, Tiffin is like a white lamb, Piggin is black like a toad and Jack is black like a cat.'

The accused women were all poor and of bad reputation. Elizabeth Bennet, also from St Osyth, was said to have used her imps to bewitch several people, including an unpleasant neighbour who called her 'old witch' and 'old whore' and killed one of her pigs with a pitchfork. According to her illegitimate daughter aged seven, Agnes Herd of Little Oakley kept imps in the form of blackbirds and cows the size of rats. Agnes got into trouble when a parson's wife who suspected her of stealing ducklings, called her 'a common harlot'. The parson's wife fell ill and one day when Agnes saw the cleric up a tree picking plums she asked him for a few. His response was less than charitable. He called her 'a vile strumpet' and sent her away empty-handed. Ursula Kemp and Elizabeth Bennet were hanged.

The tempo of witch-mania increased with more tales being told of disasters happening soon after trivial but angry incidents had

ng beggar-women. Stories of witches keeping
iety of forms were accepted as readily as the fanciful
hildren who pretended to be bewitched. Even old
m years ago could lead to charges of witchcraft. In
. a woman was charged with bewitching people to death
up to i. i years earlier. She was acquitted.

People were often quick to blame witchcraft when their animals fell
sick or died. A typical case was that of Joan Thatcher of Lawford in
Essex. She was judged guilty of killing ten sheep, three cows and a
pig owned by one farmer in April 1583, fourteen sheep, one ox, one
cow, one sow and a pig owned by another man in June, and a horse,
a cow and a pig owned by yet another in October. She died while
serving a year in prison.

In 1590 old Anne Crabbe who lived near Halstead was jailed for a
year for bewitching a neighbour 'so that her right thigh did rot off'.
A few years earlier Margaret Hacket, a widow of 60 and described as
'a notorious witch who consumed a young man to death, rotted his
bowels and backbone asunder', was hanged at Tyburn. She had
argued with a farmer who caught her taking peas from his field; with
a bailiff who hit her when she took some sticks for her fire; and with
a neighbour who refused to pay her for a pair of shoes. But many
more defendants were found not guilty as happened in 1587 to Joan
Gibson who had been charged with bewitching a windmill near
Tiptree.

In England a charge of witchcraft did not mean automatic conviction,
as was usually the case in Europe and Scotland. The ratio of
convictions to the number of accused persons varied from county to
county and though the records are incomplete, those that remain
indicate that there was always a much greater chance of acquittal than
conviction. Nine out of ten defendants were women, and the most
perilous times to face a charge of witchcraft were during the reign of
Queen Elizabeth I, the years immediately after the accession of King
James I, and worst of all, in 1645-46 when Matthew Hopkins was
active in the eastern counties.

The first case of convictions and executions resulting from the testimony of hysterical young girls was at Huntingdon in 1593. Old Mother Samuel was hanged with her husband and daughter for bewitching five daughters of Squire Throckmorton of Warboys. The Throckmortons were rich and the Samuels were poor. It was said that the Samuels had also caused the death of Lady Cromwell, second wife of Oliver Cromwell's grandfather.

The Throckmorton children continued to suffer 'fits' and they fooled an eminent doctor from Cambridge who suggested that the malady was caused by witchcraft. Mother Samuel was hectored into confessing that she kept three imps; that she had caused the death of Lady Cromwell and had bewitched the children. When pronounced guilty she showed some spirit by pleading pregnancy which made everyone in court laugh because she was getting on for 80 years old. Lady Cromwell's husband, Sir Henry, left money for a sermon to be preached in Huntingdon every year by a learned divine from Queens' College, Cambridge, on the theme of 'the detestable sin of witchcraft'.

A spate of cases of malicious fraud by children followed, sometimes with the youngsters being coached by unscrupulous adults in how to feign the symptoms of bewitchment. Thomas Darling, aged 13, counterfeited possession after an encounter with old Alice Gooderidge in a wood near Burton-upon-Trent in 1596. As she passed by the boy broke wind and called her 'the witch of Stapenhill'. She countered by declaring, 'Every boy calls me witch, but did I ever make your arse itch?' Alice was forced to confess bewitchment by being made to sit with her feet close to a fire. Her 80-year-old mother was also charged, stripped and searched for witch marks. She was found to have two teats 'like the udder on an ewe'. Asked how long she had had them she said they were warts and she had had them all her life.

A year later there was another case and again it involved a self-proclaimed exorcist by the name of John Darrell. William Somers was a disobedient Nottingham apprentice who had read about the Warboys girls and he copied their symptoms. Then along came Darrell who told him how the Burton boy had gnashed his teeth and foamed at the mouth. Thirteen women were arrested but later released and Darrell was exposed as a fraud and sent to jail.

In 1603 Mary Glover, daughter of a London merchant, fell off her stool, had fits and suffered 'vexation' after she had been 'looked earnestly upon' by Elizabeth Jackson who was sentenced to a year in jail with four appearances in the pillory. A year later another 15-year-old, Anne Gunter of North Moreton, began vomiting pins and having fits. Three women were charged and acquitted before Gunter confessed that her father had told her how to imitate the symptoms of possession as they had been described in a report of the Warboys trial. Nine women accused by a teenage boy named John Smith were hanged at Leicester in 1616 and six more were in jail awaiting trial when King James happened to visit the town. Suspecting a fraud, he ordered an inquiry and the boy's deception was revealed. The effect of James's mounting scepticism was that the number of witchcraft trials and executions declined during the closing years of his reign and it was a tendency that continued into the reign of his son, Charles I. Indeed the English witch-hunts might well have died out in the mid-17th century had it not been for the outbreak of war between King and Parliament.

Although King James was vain, lazy and extravagant, and harboured a considerable contempt for women, he was no fool and his change of attitude to witchcraft was a mark of his intelligence. When the notorious North Berwick affair had come to light in Scotland in 1590 there had been no greater believer in 'these detestable slaves of the Devil, the witches or enchanters' than James himself. That tale had begun to unfold when suspicions were aroused by the nocturnal activities of a young servant girl. Her master's harsh investigation led to several people being arrested, interrogated, tortured and condemned. The witches of North Berwick were said to have tried to shipwreck King James, and one of the accused had amazed James by repeating what he had said to his bride on their wedding night. Confessions extracted by torture drew dozens of people into the conspiracy, the root of which was a foolish plot by a wild nobleman, Francis Stuart, Earl of Bothwell. Details were given of attempts to bewitch James by using a wax image or a piece of his clothing, and there were tales of raising storms by throwing a dead cat into the sea, taking 'venom' from toads, and witches sailing to their revels in sieves.

One of the accused was schoolmaster John Fian who had developed a desire for the sister of one of his pupils. Unluckily for him the girl's mother knew a thing or two about witchcraft and she switched some hairs from her cow for those taken from her daughter's private parts. Fian's spell backfired and he was chased through the town by a lovesick cow instead of by a girl inflamed by passion. He and several others were strangled and burned.

In 1597 James published his views on witchcraft in a book called *Daemonologie*. He said his motive was to 'to resolve the doubting hearts of many; both that such assaults of Satan are most certainly practised, and that the instruments thereof [witches] merit most severely to be punished.' He condemned the opinions of two men who had written books declaring that witchcraft was a delusion - Reginald Scot 'an Englishman not ashamed in public print to deny that there can be such a thing as witchcraft', and Johan Weyer, a German court doctor whose opinions, said James, showed that he must be a witch himself.

In the year that James's book was published 23 women and a man were burned at Aberdeen. Some Scottish executions were particularly horrible. In one case in 1608 it was reported that the condemned 'were burnt alive in such a cruel manner that some died in despair, renouncing and blaspheming, and others half burnt broke out of the fire and were cast alive into it again until they were burnt to death.'

James wrote about witches being unable to sink in water saying that it was a supernatural sign of their guilt instituted by God. This, he said, was as true as the idea that if a murderer touched the body of his victim 'it will gush out of blood as if the blood were crying to the heaven for revenge.'

He regurgitated the opinion of Kramer and Sprenger that witches could not weep though you might 'threaten and torture them as you please', and in spite of the fact that women could 'shed tears at every light occasion when they will, yea, although it were dissembling like the crocodiles.' Women, he said, were frailer than men and so more easily trapped in the Devil's snares 'as was well proved to be true by the serpent's deceiving of Eve'.

Nonetheless, during the opening decades of the 17th century, the number of witch trials in England declined as the authorities became more wary of fraud and as King James's belief in witchcraft wavered. But the trials did not cease entirely. At Northampton four women and a man were hanged in 1612; a mother and daughter were executed at Bedford in 1613 and two years later Joan Hunt of Hampstead was hanged after having been acquitted twice previously. Three witches were found guilty of killing a son of the Earl of Rutland of Belvoir Castle and on the earl's tomb in Bottesford church it is written that his sons 'both died in their infancy by wicked practices and sorcery'. In 1620 William Perry, a boy from Bilston, was exposed as a liar when he claimed to be bewitched.

The trial involving the largest number of people before Hopkins began his work was also the first major witch trial in northern England. It happened in 1612 when ten witches of Pendle – most of them beggars and thieves – were executed after damning evidence had been presented against them by their own young children. At the same Lancaster assizes another fraud by a young girl was exposed and the three accused, the girl's grandmother and aunt among them, were released. Pendle was the scene of another wicked fraud twenty years later when a boy's father engineered a witch scare to cover up his thefts. The victims were pardoned although some had died in prison.

In 1616 there was a court scandal with the whiff of sorcery about it involving King James's Scottish favourite, Robert Carr, Earl of Somerset. At thirteen, Frances Howard, daughter of the Earl of Suffolk, had married Robert Devereux, Earl of Essex, who was a year older. Frances grew into an attractive woman and she decided that she preferred the attentions of the dandy Carr and a lively life at court to living with her serious-minded husband. Carr's friend, Sir Thomas Overbury, opposed the idea of her divorce and was sent to the Tower where Frances contrived to have him poisoned. There was a divorce and the lovers were married, but when Carr's fortunes began to wane the murder of Overbury returned to haunt them. First came the trial of the woman and men who had helped in the killing. The woman was Anne Turner, a widow and friend of the countess. Like most women of the time, including many at James's loose court, she believed in the effectiveness of spells and love potions. Simon Forman of Lambeth was a schoolmaster turned quack doctor, astrologer, alchemist and prophet, who, for a fee, would predict the success or otherwise of voyages and other ventures. He had supplied Frances with potions and wax images to win Carr's love and to make her husband impotent because she had not wanted him 'to enjoy her' before Carr did. Turner and others were declared guilty and hanged at Tyburn. There was a big crowd to see Mrs Turner die in her yellow starched ruff, a fashion that she had introduced. The fashion died with her that day on the scaffold. Carr and his wife were also found guilty of murder but were pardoned. When war broke out between King Charles I and Parliament it was Frances's discarded first husband who commanded Parliament's army.

In 1616 King's Lynn in Norfolk had its own very provincial and squalid scandal in which a dispute between shopkeepers about cheese ended with Mary Smith being hanged for witchery. They said she had made a sailor's fingers rot and had then sent toads and crabs to invade a shoemaker's house after he had picked up some Dutch cheeses at bargain prices. She had cursed widow Elizabeth Hancock by wishing 'a pox to light upon her' so that a few hours later Elizabeth had 'felt a sudden weakness in all the parts of her body'. Elizabeth Hancock's father went to a cunning man for help and was told to bake a 'witch cake' using his daughter's urine, then to spread a treacle-like ointment on the cake and apply it to Elizabeth's body, front and back. It failed to do her much good because three years later it was said she 'yet lives, but in no confirmed health, nor perfect soundness of body.' The mayor and council commissioned the town's Puritan vicar, Alexander Roberts, to write a book about the affair and his *A Treatise of Witchcraft* may well have been another of the books which influenced Hopkins. It repeated many of the stale old tales about witches declaring that for every male witch there were a hundred female witches and it was all because women had slippery tongues and an 'unsatiable desire for revenge'.

The number of witch trials dwindled to almost insignificance in the early years of the reign of Charles I. From his accession in 1625 until the outbreak of the English Civil War in 1642 there were remarkably few witch executions. The ratio of acquittals rose as judges and juries became less inclined to believe many of the wild stories. Sometimes even those who re-appeared before the courts were exonerated.

But witch-mania resurfaced soon after the start of the civil war with both sides using it in their propaganda. Some soldiers from the army led by the Earl of Essex were fruit-picking near Newbury one day in 1643 when they saw a woman apparently walking on water 'with as much ease and firmness as if one should walk or trample on the earth'. In fact she was crossing the river on a raft. When they tried to shoot her she caught the bullets and chewed them and another shot rebounded off her. She was subdued after they drew blood 'from forth the veins that cross the temples of the head' and after she had predicted a victory for Parliament's army they despatched her with a pistol shot.

Prince Rupert's pet poodle was said to be a Hebrew-speaking 'witch, sorceress and enemy to Parliament' which would catch bullets in its teeth. The unfortunate dog was killed at the battle of Marston Moor by a 'valiant soldier who had skill in necromancy'.

Detecting the Devil's Darlings

argaret Simons of Brenchley in Kent had a little dog and one day it barked at the vicar's son. The boy was an unpleasant character and he pulled out a knife and chased the dog back into her house. When Mrs Simons rebuked him an argument developed and a few days later the boy fell ill. His father, a man who thought God would not 'visit his children with sickness' and who was 'fondly besotted' in his belief in witchcraft, decided that the boy's malady was caused by witchery. Then when the vicar lost his voice and could not preach he blamed that on enchantment too.

But Mrs Simons told a very different story. She said that many good people in the village suspected that the vicar's hoarseness was the result of 'the French pox' and refused to have any dealings with him until he could produce a certificate signed by two London doctors saying that his voice problem was caused by another less embarrassing disease. In 1581, at the instigation of the hoarse vicar and other 'malicious persons', Mrs Simons stood trial for witchcraft. Reginald Scot, who met and spoke to many of the main characters in the affair, wrote, 'The name of a witch is so odious and her power so feared among the common people that if the honestest body living chance to be arraigned thereupon, she shall hardly escape condemnation.' And Mrs Simons would have been condemned too if 'one of the jury had not been wiser than the others.' The tale of Mrs Simons and the vicar of Brenchley, said Scot, showed how 'the fables of witchcraft have taken so fast hold and deep root in the heart of man.' In a book published in 1584 he poured scorn on many of the commonly held ideas about witchery and declared that the book by Kramer and Sprenger was 'nothing but stinking lies'.

One of the fraudulent cases of 'diabolical witchcraft and ventriloquie' which Scot witnessed happened in 1574 at Westwell in Kent. Mildred Norington, a servant girl aged 17, was said to be possessed and two ministers led an attempt to expel the evil spirit. The possessing devil went 'through all his delays [such] as roaring, crying, striving and gnashing of teeth and otherwise with terrible countenances and was so strong in the maid that four men could scarce hold her down and this continued by the space of two hours.' Eventually the demon was banished, but only after it had threatened to tear everyone to pieces and had admitted that it took meat, drink and corn to a certain old Alice of Westwell with whom it normally lived in a bottle. 'How could mother Alice escape condemnation and hanging being arraigned upon this evidence?' asked Scot.

But the girl's fraud was discovered when she was questioned by local magistrates. Scot commented, 'Neither was her confession won according to the form of the Spanish inquisition, to wit through extremity of tortures, nor yet by guile, nor by presumptions, but through wise and perfect trial of every circumstance the illusion was manifestly disclosed: not so (I say) as witches are commonly condemned; to wit, through malicious accusations, by guesses, presumptions and extorted confessions contrary to sense and possibility, and for such actions as they can show no trial nor example before the wise, either by direct or indirect means; but after due trial she showed her feats, illusions and trances. Now compare this wench with the witch of Endor and you shall see that both the cousenages may be done by one art.'

Those who believed in witchery countered scepticism like Scot's by declaring that it must be true because witches confessed to sending their imps to torment people, blast crops, raise storms and sink ships while also admitting suckling those imps, meeting Satan in various forms and sealing their pacts with blood in return for promises of money, food or some other small improvement in their standard of life. Scot's response was to say, 'If they [witches] find by themselves or by their devils could trouble the elements we should never have fair weather. If they could kill men, children or cattle they would spare none, but would destroy and kill whole countries and households. If they could transfer corn from their neighbour's field into their own none of them would be poor, none other should be rich. If they could transform themselves and others, as it is most constantly affirmed, of what a number of apes and owls should there be of us!

'If it were true that witches confess or that all writers write or that witchmongers report, or that fools believe, we should never have butter in the churn, nor cow in the close, nor corn in the field, nor fair weather abroad, nor health within doors. Or if that which is contained in Malleus Maleficarum, Bodin [Jean Bodin was a French philosopher and judge who presided over many witch trials] or in the pamphlets late set forth in English, of witches executions, should be true in those things that witches are said to confess, what creature could live in security? No prince should be able to reign or live in the land. One old witch might overthrow an army royal and then what need we any guns, or wild fire, or any other instruments of war? A witch might supply all wants and accomplish a prince's will in this behalf, even without charge and bloodshed of his people.

'They [witches] use incestuous adultery with spirits. Answer, this is a stale ridiculous lie. They boil infants, after they have murdered them unbaptised, until their flesh is made potable. Answer, this is untrue, incredible and impossible. They eat the flesh and drink the blood of men and children openly. Answer, then are they kin to the anthropophagi [man-eaters] and cannibals. But I believe never an honest man in England nor in France, will affirm that he has seen any of these persons that are said to be witches do so; if they should, I believe it would poison them. They kill men with poison. Answer, let them be hanged for their labour. They kill men's cattle. Answer, then let an action of trespass be brought against them for so doing. They bewitch men's corn and bring hunger and barrenness into the country; they ride and fly in the air, bring storms, make tempests etc. Answer, then will I worship them as gods; for those be not the works of man, nor yet of witch: as I have elsewhere proved. They use venery with a devil called incubus, even when they lie in bed with their husbands, and have children by them, which become the best witches. Answer, this is the last lie, very ridiculous.'

Scot's book recorded many superstitious beliefs of his day such as carrying a piece of coral stopped you getting drunk. He noted a charm that would give a pregnant woman an easy delivery. It was 'throw over the house where a woman in travail lies, a stone or any other thing that has killed three living creatures, namely a man, a wild boar and a she bear.' For the falling illness [epilepsy] it was proposed that the patient 'drink in the night at a spring water out of a skull of one that has been slain or eat a pig killed with a knife that slew a man.'

It was Scot who noted the superstition that nailing a horseshoe to your door kept witches at bay. Later when witch-mania was dying away, a foreigner remarked, 'Having often observed a horseshoe nailed to the threshold of a door among the meaner sort of people, I asked several what was the reason of it; they gave me several different answers but the most general was that they were put there to keep out witches. 'Tis true they laugh when they say this, but yet they do not laugh at it altogether; for they believe there may be some secret virtue concealed in it.'

As well as the idea of the lucky horseshoe, we have been bequeathed many other superstitions from those days. It was said that 'on meeting a supposed witch, it is advisable, whilst passing her, to clench both hands, doubling the thumbs beneath the fingers: this will prevent her having a power to injure the person so doing.' Condemned felons such as witches took their last steps beneath the ladder of the gallows tree so according to superstition walking under a ladder brings very bad luck.

A bride used to be advised to put a silver sixpence in her shoes for the first few days of her married life 'lest the malignant glance of a disappointed lover's eye should have a physical effect on her constitution', and they said a witch who turned herself into a hare could only be killed by a silver bullet. The hare was associated with witchcraft because it was claimed that the animal had been sacred to a pagan goddess whose feast had been celebrated at Easter time. Another belief was that iron protected against witches and fairies. One story told how a Suffolk blacksmith was helping a milkmaid with the churning one day but the butter would not come so he began to suspect witchery. He threw a piece of hot iron into the churn 'upon which a poor labourer employed in carrying dung in the yard, cried out in a terrible manner, 'They have killed me, they have killed me,' still keeping his hand upon his back intimating where the pain was, and died upon the spot. They took off the poor man's clothes and found to their great surprise, the mark of the iron that was heated and thrown into the churn deeply impressed upon his back.'

It was said that people whose eyebrows joined were probably witches because it had been noticed that old women condemned as witches had eyebrows like that, and 'they whose hair of the eyebrows do touch or meet together, of all are the worst. They do show that he or she is a wicked person given to unlawful and naughty arts.'

Continental demonologists accepted the idea of lycanthropy – the ability to turn into a wolf – but it found no real place in English witchcraft. Nor did the idea of covens, sabbats, mass sexual orgies or child sacrifice. And seldom were there reports of English witches flying on broomsticks or changing into animals. In a rare instance when flying was mentioned a sceptical judge remarked that as far as he knew flying on a broomstick was not against the laws of England. The problem for English lawmakers and judges was that while everyone thought they knew what witchcraft was, it was difficult to define a witch in strict legal terms. Demonologists were usually happy to say it was 'a certain art whereby with the assistance of the Devil or evil spirits, some wonders may be wrought which exceed the common understanding of men.'

Scot said this was nonsense and declared that the 'mischiefs' blamed on witches also happened in places where there were no witches, and even continued when all the local witches had been hanged. 'Why then should we attribute such effects to that cause [witchcraft], which being taken away, happen nevertheless?' he asked.

While theologians and learned men conjectured about the nature and source of the supposed power of witches with many of them saying that witches themselves had no occult powers, judges were often reluctant to condemn a defendant to death on charges other than having caused death by bewitchment. Matthew Hopkins was to argue that neither the Devil nor the witch actually caused death. He said that the Devil, being more than 6,000 years old, knew if someone was ill and caused a quarrel between that person and a witch. The Devil then promised to murder the person and when the victim eventually died of disease the witch assumed that death had been caused by Satan's hand.

Witches were supposed to bewitch in a variety of ways. They could do it by cursing, by potions [witches and sorcerers had long been feared as poisoners]; by making images or by taking some hair or something that had been worn by their victim. They also knotted cords to cause impotency, they used the 'evil eye' [fascination], sent their imps on evil errands or buried a toad or snake under the threshold. The high rate of infant mortality meant that midwives were obvious targets for suspicions because witches were said to be under orders to kill at least one baby each month. It was alleged that they often did it by making it appear that the child had been accidentally smothered during the night while sleeping with its parents.

The Devil delighted in making men impotent. This was done by disturbing a man's imagination so that a woman seemed hideous to him; by suppressing his vigour, or by making him believe he had lost his penis. How was a man to know if he had been bewitched into impotency? 'When he is no way stirred and can never perform the act, this is a sign of natural frigidity; but when he is stirred yet cannot perform it is a sign of witchcraft' was the Church's explanation. Scot listed several 'magical cures for them bewitched in their privities' – 'Eating of a haggister [magpie] helps one bewitched in that member. The smoke of the tooth of a dead man. To anoint a man's body with the gall of crow. To fill a quill with quicksilver and lay the same under the cushion where such a one sits, or else to put under the threshold of the door of the house or chamber where he dwells. To spit into your own bosom, if you be so bewitched, is very good. To piss through a wedding ring.'

One way of ending bewitchment that was recommended by cunning men involved boiling the victim's urine. This is one version of remedy. 'Take two horseshoes, heat them red hot, and nail one on the threshold of the door, but quench the other in the urine of the party bewitched; then set the urine over the fire in a pot or pipkin and put the horseshoes into it. Make the urine boil with a little salt put into it and three horseshoe nails, until it is almost all consumed. What is not boiled away, toss into the fire. Keep the horseshoes and nails in a clean paper or cloth, and use the same manner three times. It will be more effectual if done at the change or full of the moon.' Simon Forman, the Elizabethan astrologer and quack doctor who was popular with the top rank of society, suggested burning a handful of thatch or a tile taken from the roof of the witch's house.

A favourite trick of witches, so it was believed, was to make an image of the victim out of wax or clay and then roast it or stab it. King James wrote 'that by the roasting thereof, the persons that they bear the name of, may be continually melted or dried away by continual sickness.' Scot described the process like this. 'Make an image in his name whom you would hurt or kill of new virgin wax, under the right arm poke whereof place a swallow's heart, and the liver under the left; then hang about the neck a new thread in a new needle pricked into the member which you would have hurt, with the rehearsal of certain words. Sometimes these images are made of brass, and then the hand is placed where the foot should be, and the foot where the hand, and the face downward.

'For a greater mischief, the like image is made in the form of a man or woman upon whose head is written the certain name of the party, and on his or her ribs these words, Ailif, casyl, zaza, hit mel meltat; then the same must be buried. Otherwise, in the dominion of Mars, two images must be prepared, one of wax, the other of the earth of a dead man; each image must have in his hand a sword wherewith a man has been slain. In both must be written certain peculiar characters, and then must they be hid in a certain place. Otherwise, to obtain a woman's love, an image must be made in the hour of Venus of virgin wax, in the name of the beloved, whereupon a character is written and is warmed at a fire, and in doing thereof the name of some angel must be mentioned.'

Women who wanted to stop demons making love to them in the guise of handsome young men were advised to put some hypericon on their breasts or scatter it around the house because 'it is hateful to all their kind'. Vervain and dill also worked according to the rhyme 'trefoil, vervain, John's wort, dill, hinder witches in their will.'

A ridiculous tale of the 'lecheries most horrible and very filthy and fabulous actions and passions of witches' which Scot wearied of repeating concerned a priest 'fair and fat and of an excellent complexion' who became 'skin and bone' as the result of a woman's nightly sexual attentions. The exhausted priest went to a cunning witch who told him 'the next morning about the dawning of the day, he should piss and immediately should cover the pisspot.' The effect was that the witch came to his house and 'complained of a grief in her bladder and that she could not piss. But I [the priest] could neither by fair nor foul means obtain at her hands that she would leave molesting me by night; but she keeps her old custom, determining by these filthy means to despatch me.'

Sexual encounters with the Devil featured in numerous confessions but it was far from being a pleasant activity because, according to some witches, the Devil had the habit of appearing as a huge black monster with an enormous penis as cold as ice. One old Suffolk witch reported her disappointment when he came to her in the shape of a handsome young man but was 'colder and heavier and could not perform as a man.'

There were many ways of protecting against witches. Hawthorn, yew, rowan or even a scattering of broad beans was said to keep a household safe. Seven elder trees in the garden made spells impotent and it was said a bay tree 'resists witchcraft very potently, neither witch nor devil, thunder nor lightning will hurt a man in the place where a bay tree is.' Coral 'preserves such as bear it from fascination or bewitching, and in this respect they are hung about children's necks, and to hang an egg laid on Ascension Day in the roof of the house, preserves the same from all hurts.' Witches could not enter where two sticks were placed on the ground in the form of a cross, and ashes of burnt rosemary sprinkled in the hearth warded off the evil eye. A holly hedge or mistletoe above a door protected against fire, storms and the evil eye. A bat carried around the house three times and then nailed to a window was a charm against all sorts of sorcery. Sprinkling some salt in a fire or burying frogs' livers and toads' hearts in bottles near a church was supposed to destroy a witch's power. To know if someone was bewitched it was recommended that 'you must hold molten lead over the sick body and pour it into a porringer full of water; and then, if there appear upon the lead any image you may then know the party is bewitched.'

An all-purpose counter to spells was to 'spit into the shoe of your right foot before you put it on.' Splashing your house with water taken from a stream 'over which the living and the dead pass' and in which a piece of silver had been left overnight was a remedy for witches' curses. These were no more bizarre than many medical 'cures' of the time which included 'against the biting of a mad dog take pills made of the skull of one that is hanged' and 'moss growing on a human skull, if dried, powdered and taken as snuff, will cure headache.'

Another remedy for witchery was to 'hang a stone over the afflicted person's bed, which stone has naturally such a hole in it as wherein a string may be put through it, and be hanged over the diseased or bewitched party; be it man, woman or horse.' These stones, sometimes called hag stones, were also said to prevent nightmares and stop witches riding the horses at night.

Other ways of unbewitching were 'to spit into the pisspot where you have made water' or 'strike a bewitched child seven times on the face and upon the navel with the heart of a black cat, then roast the heart and give it to eat seven nights at bed meal [supper] and it shall be well, but the cat must be seven years old and the seventh dropped at birth.' Blood from such a heart thrown on a witch's doorstep at night was said to cause her 'a sore and great pain in her belly.'

One way of forcing a witch to reveal her identity when cattle were killed by witchery was to drag the bowels of the dead beast into your kitchen and put them over a fire. As they got hot so the witch's entrails would begin to hurt her and she would come to the house and try to snatch away one of the hot coals because that would end her torment. Many people believed a spell could be lifted if a witch was made to bleed by scratching her face, and one eminent physician advised that all shells of boiled eggs should be turned upside down and broken to prevent witches using them as boats. Another wild notion was that captured witches should be carried in a basket or on a plank to prevent them touching the ground because if they were allowed to do so 'they would free themselves and strike many people dead with lightning.'

Malice and spite often motivated a charge of witchcraft and in some Scottish churches a locked chest was provided in which anonymous accusers could put a piece of paper bearing the name of a supposed witch. 'And thus,' said Scot, 'the accuser need not be known nor shamed with the reproach of slander or malice to his poor neighbour.' Hopkins concentrated on three ways of discovering witches – searching for marks on the body, 'swimming', and 'watching and keeping'. Watching and keeping was tantamount to torture. It involved keeping the victim awake for several days and nights while sometimes also making them walk up and down until their feet were blistered and total exhaustion overtook them. Depriving them of food and drink was another tactic. John Gaule, a parson from near Huntingdon, described what was done. 'Having taken the suspected witch, she is placed in the middle of a room upon a stool or table, cross-legged, or in some other uneasy posture, to which if she submits not she is then bound with cords, there is she watched and kept without meat or sleep for the space of twenty-four hours for, they say, within that time they shall see her imp come and suck. A little hole is likewise made in the door for the imp to come in at; and lest it might come in some less discernible shape, they that watch are taught to be ever and anon sweeping the room, and if they see any spiders or flies, to kill them. And if they cannot kill them when they may be seen they are her imps.' Hopkins' associate John Stearne denied that the object was 'to use violence or extremity' to force a confession. He said the motive was to isolate the suspects from their usual company of 'idle persons' so that 'godly divines and others might discourse with them'. Then by 'laying the heinousness of their sins to them and in what condition they are in without repentance, and telling them the subtleties of the Devil and the mercies of God, these ways will bring them to confession without extremity. It will make them break into confession hoping for mercy.' He added that the isolation was also intended to see if any of the witch's imps came to her.

Experts said two sorts of marks were to be found on a witch's body. The Devil's mark was like a birthmark and said to have been made by the Devil's claw. 'That mark is not always of the same shape: sometimes it is the image of a hare, a toad's leg, a spider, a puppy, a dormouse. It is imprinted on the most hidden parts of the body: with men under the eyelids or the armpits or lips, on the shoulder, the fundament, or somewhere else: with women it is usually on the breasts or the privy parts.' The witch's mark was the teat or bigg at which her imps were suckled. Witch-hunters did not always bother about the distinction declaring that both marks were insensitive to pain.

It was the job of witch-prickers to put such marks to the test. Because the prickers were paid by results it was a trade that attracted unscrupulous rogues and one of their tricks was to use a bodkin with a retractable point. One who was hired to search for witches at Newcastle and 'to have twenty shillings a piece for all he could condemn' had fourteen women and one man hanged although they all protested their innocence. The man was later arrested in Scotland where 'upon the gallows he confessed that he had been the death of above 220 women in England and Scotland for the gain of twenty shillings a piece, beseeched forgiveness and was executed.'

Ordeal by water was an ancient method of establishing guilt or innocence and although it was unlawful the test came into widespread use. The victim would be bound left thumb to right big toe and right thumb to left big toe and then tipped into a pond or river with a rope tied around the waist. If she floated it was a sign of guilt. If she sank, perhaps drowning in the process, it indicated innocence.

Although a wholehearted believer in witchcraft, Puritan preacher William Perkins was unconvinced by this argument. He wrote, 'To justify the casting of a witch into the water, it is alleged that having made a covenant with the Devil she has renounced her baptism, and hereupon there grows an antipathy between her and water. This allegation serves to no purpose: for all water is not the water of baptism, but that only which is used in the very act of baptism.'

Such theological precision did not stop the test being used and for more than one hundred years after the scrapping of the witchcraft laws, people were still thrown into ponds to see if they would float. Indeed early in the 18th century the practice prompted one Lord Chief Justice to issue the warning that 'if any man hereafter uses that ungodly trial and the party tried is drowned, neither King James's Book, nor any other past precedents will save them from a halter.' In 1751 at Tring an old man and his wife were stripped, tied and tossed into a pond by a mob and when the woman floated a chimneysweep waded in and pushed her under with a stick. The two old people died of their ill treatment and the sweep was hanged for murder.

It was to counter criticism of his methods that Hopkins published his pamphlet *The Discovery of Witches* in 1647. How could he justify the 'abominable, inhumane, and unmerciful trial of these poor creatures by tying them, and heaving them into the water; a trial not allowable by law or conscience?' He admitted that some suspects found with teats had been 'so served and floated, others that had none were tried with them and sunk.' He blamed it on the Devil's deceit. 'For first the Devil's policy is great in persuading many to come of their own accord to be tried, persuading them their marks are so close [well hidden] they shall not be found out, so as divers have come 10 or 12 miles to be searched of their own accord, and hanged for their labour, as one Meggs, a baker did, who lived within seven miles of Norwich and was hanged at Norwich Assizes for witchcraft, then when they found that the Devil tells them false they reflect on him, and he, as 40 have confessed, advises them to be swum, and tells them they shall sink and be cleared that way, then when they be tried that way and float, they see the Devil deceives them again, and has so laid open his treacheries.'

Hopkins asserted that he never used the swimming test as evidence against his victims and repeated King James's opinion that a witch would not sink because 'witches deny their baptism when they covenant with the Devil, water being the sole element thereof, and therefore when they be heaved into the water, the water refuses to receive them into her bosom, they being such miscreants to deny their baptism, and suffers them to float as the froth of the sea which the water will not receive, but casts it up and down till it comes to the earthy element the shore and there leaves it to consume.'

How could Hopkins tell the difference between natural skin blemishes and witches' marks? His answer was by their position, their insensibility to pain 'feeling neither pin, needle, awl thrust through them' and the 'variations and mutations of these marks into several forms.'

As for denying his victims sleep, Hopkins said it was done in the early days of his witch-hunting when it was 'not only thought fitting, but enjoined in Essex and Suffolk by the magistrates, with this intention only, because they being kept awake would be more the active to call their imps in open view the sooner to their help, which oftentimes have so happened; and never or seldom did any witch ever complain in the time of their keeping for want of rest.' As for being 'extraordinarily walked till their feet was blistered and so forced through that cruelty to confess', the reason for that was that when the suspect was 'suffered so to couch, immediately come their familiars into the room and scratch the watchers and hearten on the witch.'

Witchcraft beliefs became so entangled with illogical claims and unfounded and often contradictory religious dogmas that defence against an accusation of witchery could be impossible. As Bishop Francis Hutchinson pointed out, 'The fantastic doctrines that support the vulgar opinions of witchcraft rob us of all the defences that God and nature have placed for our security against false accusation. For in other cases, when wicked or mistaken people charge us with crimes of which we are not guilty, we clear ourselves by showing that at that time we were at home or in some other place about our honest business. But in prosecutions for witchcraft that most natural and just defence is a mere jest. For if any wicked person affirms, or any crack-brained girl imagines, or any lying spirit makes her believe that she sees an old woman or other person pursuing her in her visions, the defenders of the vulgar witchcraft tack an imaginary unproved compact to the deposition and hang the accused parties for things that they were doing when they were perhaps asleep in their beds, or saying their prayers, or perhaps in the accuser's own possession with double irons upon them.'

Anyway, said the sceptics, if the Devil promised witches wealth and a life of ease why were they such poor and beggarly creatures? The twisted logic of the witch-hunters was that the Devil showed his contempt for God by buying witches at the lowest possible price and he then stopped them from becoming conspicuous by their wealth! Reginald Scot made the wry comment, 'Among us we think them bewitched that wax suddenly poor and not them that grow hastily rich.'

The Witch-hunt Begins

*T*he worst witch-hunt in English history had its roots in the Essex port of Manningtree during the dark midwinter days around Christmas 1644.

It was a bleak and depressing time. The seemingly interminable civil war between King and Parliament was well into its third year. The Puritans who dominated Parliament had banned all Christmas celebrations, and strict religious observance was the order of the day. Theatres were shut, sports were banned, and drinking and dancing had been wrathfully declared to be sinful. Even the maypole had been outlawed as 'a heathenish vanity.'

Across the eastern counties men were being recruited for a new Roundhead army and in towns and villages throughout the land people were grumbling more than ever about high taxes and rising prices. Parliament had enlisted the Scots as their allies in the war against the King and every man over 18 was supposed to have sworn to uphold the Solemn League and Covenant because that was the price of Scottish assistance. The Scots wanted to abolish the rites, traditions and structures of the Church of England and refashion it on their own Presbyterian model. That included 'the discovery [exposure] of all such as have been or shall be incendiaries, malignants or evil instruments by hindering the reformation of religion, dividing the king from his people, or one of the kingdoms from another or making faction or parties amongst the people'. They also wanted to abolish 'archbishops, bishops, their chancellors and commissaries, deans, deans and chapters, archdeacons and all other ecclesiastical officers depending on that hierarchy, superstition, heresy, schism, profaneness and whatsoever shall be found to be contrary to sound doctrine and the power of godliness'. In East Anglia many village parsons had been marked out as 'malignants, drunkards and dumb-dogs', and replaced by ministers considered to be of a more godly character.

In 1643 Parliament had ordered 'the utter demolishing, removing and taking away of all monuments of superstition or idolatry' from churches. Norwich cathedral had been sacked by a mob led by some Puritan fanatics so that it was left 'open on all sides to be filled with musketeers drinking and smoking as freely as if it had turned alehouse.' The religious fanaticism of some was such that a Norfolk squire of Puritan sympathies deplored their activities as 'the oppression is very odious, their fury in churches detestable.' In 1644 William Dowsing had led a squad of soldiers into dozens of Suffolk churches to smash the picture windows, topple the crosses, pull up the memorial brasses and rip out the altar rails.

It was the time of the Puritan ascendancy when religion was intruded into every aspect of life. The 'saints' as the Puritans were derisively called, believed they were living in truly apocalyptic times. They searched for signs that God was blessing their efforts to make England the 'new Jerusalem' while also being alert to any evidence that witches, the Devil's own 'evil instruments', were working their wickedness. To them the civil war itself was the work of the Devil.

In Manningtree the mood had remained cheerless and sombre during those short midwinter days, particularly in the home of the town's tailor, John Rivet. There the continuing violent fits suffered by his wife had made John suspect that something very unnatural was going on, and when he talked about it with his friends they also voiced fears that witchery was being practised in their town.

They remembered the previous summer when Richard Edwards' infant son John had died after having strange fits. Edwards, a prosperous merchant of the Puritan persuasion, was an important man in the community and a firm friend of Hopkins and Stearne, and the death of his son had occurred only a few days after the death of Henry Woolvett's young daughter. And one moonlight night, Matthew Hopkins, a man known to the local magistrate as 'a very honest man who would not speak an untruth', had encountered several imps in the shape of black rabbits belonging to that notorious beldam, Anne West. That had happened in the nearby village of Lawford which was where Prudence Hart who seemed 'well and healthful' one minute, had suffered a miscarriage after walking half a mile to church on a cold Sunday in February.

March 1645 was a month of great winds and gales, and John Rivet decided it was time to settle the matter of his wife's ill health. He travelled the eight miles to Hadleigh in Suffolk to seek the opinion of Goodwife Hovey, the local cunning woman. She quickly confirmed his fears, declaring that two women had cursed his wife. Rivet immediately identified one of the miscreants as Elizabeth Clarke, a one-legged old hag whose evil reputation came from the belief that several of her kin – her mother among them – had been put to death for witchcraft and murder.

When Rivet returned home and reported what had happened, it reinforced the suspicions held by Hopkins, Stearne and other leading citizens that a gang of witches was active in and around Manningtree. Those suspicions had grown out of the events of the previous year and other more recent experiences involving Clarke and her friends. They decided it was time for action.

Unfortunately for the would-be witch-hunters, the tailor's story was flimsy indeed and was corroborated only by the word of a notorious cunning woman, and in the opinion of reputable authorities on witchcraft, a cunning woman and a cursing witch were as like as two peas from the same pod. Hopkins and his friends recognised that the tailor's story alone would not persuade the magistrates to issue arrest warrants. They needed evidence so strong that the justices would have no alternative but to act.

Handbooks for the guidance of magistrates indicated the tactics they should use. According to Michael Dalton's book *The Country Justice*, evidence of keeping familiars, and having teats or Devil's marks on the body were 'main points to discover and convict these witches, for they prove fully that those witches have a familiar and made a league with the Devil.' But even more damning was a witch's 'own voluntary confession of the hurt they have done or of the giving of their souls to the Devil, and of the spirits which they have, how many, how they call them and how they came by them.' A confession 'exceeded all other evidence.'

So evidence of imps, or of teats and marks in a witch's 'secretest parts', or a confession were guarantees of conviction. Hopkins also noted another indication of guilt listed in the book. This was 'if the suspect be proved to have been heard to call upon their spirit, or to talk to them, or of them, or have offered them to others'. Hopkins seized on these indicators to begin the witch-hunt.

The days that followed the tailor's visit to the cunning woman were ones of feverish activity as the would-be witch-hunters laid their plans. How tongues must have wagged in Manningtree with talk of witches!

Then one night Hopkins heard Elizabeth Clarke calling to her cats and dogs. It was the chance he had been waiting for. To Hopkins it was not an old woman calling to her pets but one old witch telling her imps to go to another old witch. That was justification enough for him to detain her and have her searched for teats and marks made by the Devil's claw.

Hopkins described what happened. He wrote, 'In March 1645 he [Hopkins] had some seven or eight of that horrible sect of witches living in the town were he lived, a town in Essex called Manningtree with divers [several] other adjacent witches of other towns, who every six weeks in the night (being always on the Friday night) had their meeting close by his house, and had their several solemn sacrifices there offered to the Devil, one of which this discoverer heard speaking to her imps one night, and bid them go to another witch, who was thereupon apprehended and searched by women who had many years known the Devil's marks, and found to have three teats about her which honest women have not.'

Elizabeth Clarke was searched by Mary Phillips and Frances Mills, two women for whom the body searching of suspected witches became almost a career over the next weeks and months. The teats they claimed to have found on their old victim were cause enough to have the matter put before magistrates, but a few days later when two justices sat down to take the first step in the legal process and to consider whether this matter of witchcraft should go any further, the clinching evidence was not about Clarke's calls to her imps, the body search for the teats by which she fed them, or the tailor's story of his wife's woes. The evidence that suddenly gave the witch-hunt new and urgent legal impetus came from a young woman by the name of Rebecca West.

On Friday March 21, 1645, with the fingers of a cold wind reaching into every nook and cranny of the room, John Rivet stood in front of two justices of the peace. He told them about his wife's long and lingering illness, and of his suspicions concerning old Elizabeth Clarke. The magistrates listening to him that day were Sir Harbottle Grimstone and Sir Thomas Bowes, two men whose religious opinions were very much in tune with the beliefs of the would-be witch-finders. What they heard from the tailor's lips would have made their Puritan hackles rise. But that was as nothing compared to their reaction when they heard the evidence of the star-witness, the self-confessed witch Rebecca West. She was the daughter of Anne West, a widow who lived at Lawford about a mile from Manningtree, and whose imps Hopkins had met one night in the shape of black rabbits.

Rebecca's testimony was the catalyst that set the witch-hunt in motion. Without it the witch-hunt would never have started and Matthew Hopkins may well have lived out a much longer but thoroughly unremarkable life.

Rebecca's story – and it was one she repeated several times with some variations – was far more devastating than that told by Master Rivet. As well as confessing her own witchery, she named five other women, including her own mother, as witches. She told how they met together to plot their revenge and she described the evil deeds that their imps performed. She said the ringleader was none other than Elizabeth Clarke, the toothless old cripple suspected by tailor Rivet of bewitching his wife. She named the other witches as her widowed mother, Anne West; mason's wife Helen Clarke and labourer's wife Elizabeth Gooding, both from Manningtree; and widow Anne Leech from nearby Mistley. [Anne Leech and Helen Clarke were mother and daughter.]

Rebecca told the magistrates that towards the end of February [in another account it was around April 1644] she had met the other women at Elizabeth Clarke's home and there they had each instructed their imps on the wicked deeds they wanted them to do. Clarke had asked her familiar to scare Richard Edwards' horse as it crossed a bridge so that he would be thrown and killed. Gooding wanted revenge because she was suspected of killing a horse belonging to Robert Taylor. Helen Clarke wanted her imp to kill a hog, and Anne Leech asked her familiar to injure a cow. Anne West asked 'that she might be freed from all her enemies and have no trouble'. Rebecca concluded her confession by saying that she had asked her spirit to lame Prudence, the wife of Thomas Hart. A few days later Prudence had suffered her miscarriage.

The part played by Rebecca West in the Manningtree witch-hunt raises many questions. Why did she make such a confession, one that by all accounts was a genuinely voluntary one? Why did she put herself and her mother in danger of ending their lives on the gallows? [Anne West did indeed die on the gallows four months later.] What were the motives that led her to do what she did, and perhaps more importantly, what was her relationship with Hopkins and the witch-hunters? From their point of view she was the ideal witness. She came from a family long tainted by suspicions of witchcraft. Some years previously Anne West had been held in jail on a charge of witchery, and according to Stearne, she had drawn her daughter into witchcraft 'after a strange manner'. There is no evidence that Rebecca West was subjected to the rough treatment or intimidation that others later suffered at the hands of the witch-hunters. She was not 'swum' or kept without sleep or sustenance.

The Wests were well known to Hopkins and the Puritan clique which dominated Manningtree society. The mother was a known associate of the old beldam Elizabeth Clarke and, as far as the more fundamentalist John Stearne was concerned, she was false in both her faith and her practice of religion. He wrote, 'The mother of the said Rebecca West, and many others which by their carriage seemed to be very religious people and would constantly repair to all sermons near them, yet notwithstanding all their shows of religion, there appeared some of these probabilities, whereby they were suspected and so searched and so by that means discovered and made known.'

And as for Rebecca, certainly she may not have been the chaste and innocent young maiden that some have suggested. She had survived the months when her mother has been held in jail, and in a confession to John Edes, a cleric who knew the family, she said she had been sexually active for seven years. There is no reason to assume that this was a figure picked at random. Indeed the section of her confession to Edes about her 'familiarity with the Devil' perhaps holds several clues to her motivation.

For most women the only way to escape a life of grinding poverty was marriage. It was an aspiration that even the toothless and crippled octogenarian Elizabeth Clarke clung to. But the granting of sexual favours to a man has never been a guarantee of marriage. Nonetheless, that is what Rebecca did.

A feature of the Hopkins' witch-hunt is the emphasis he and Stearne placed on revelations of witches' supposed sexual relations with the Devil. What was confessed was often fantasy, and sometimes it was the retelling of real sexual encounters with men in the past. Let us examine more closely the words attributed to Rebecca by cleric John Edes. He said, 'Rebecca West confessed that about seven years since she began to have familiarity with the Devil by the instigation of her mother, Anne West; who [the Devil] has appeared to the said Rebecca at several times in divers shapes, at one time in the likeness of a proper young man who desired of her that he might have the same familiarity with her that others that appeared to her before had had, promising that if she would he would then do for the said Rebecca what she desired and avenge her on her enemies.'

In April 1645, only a few days after the start of the witch-hunt, Hopkins visited Rebecca in Colchester Castle where she was being held and subsequently he made a report of that meeting to the magistrates. According to Hopkins she repeated the tale about going with her mother to Elizabeth Clarke's house. But added to that story was her admission that the Devil had later appeared to her as she was going to bed and he had told her that he would marry her. They then went through a mock marriage ceremony in which the Devil promised 'to be her loving husband till death, and to avenge her of her enemies.' There was no mention of this sexual encounter in her original confession and if the Devil is substituted by 'a proper young man' such as Rebecca desired we have a description of the classic seduction technique used by lusting young men on love-struck young women in every age. A few days later came the confession to Edes in which Rebecca is said to have confessed a 'familiarity' with the Devil over seven years during which he had appeared to her in many guises. Why would Hopkins wish to further blacken Rebecca's character with details of her 'carnal copulation' with the Devil? Why, having obtained Rebecca's confession to a capital offence, did Hopkins visit her in Colchester Castle to get a second and more damning confession? Indeed, it seems that he visited her in the decaying old castle more than once because another account states that after she had admitted 'carnal copulation with the Devil' at her trial, she was 'asked divers questions by a gentleman that did speak several times with her before and afterward (giving her godly and comfortable instructions)'

Where do these hints and speculations lead? Could it be that the Manningtree witch-hunt gave Hopkins the chance to hide a dark secret? Consider now the curious statement delivered by the magistrate, Sir Thomas Bowes, at Anne West's trial. It concerned the encounter between Hopkins and several imps in the shape of rabbits one moonlight night. What was 'a very honest man of Manningtree who would not speak an untruth' doing abroad in Lawford at four o'clock in the morning? Could it be that the tale of imps and a face-to-face meeting with Anne West at her door was intended to put a confrontation between Hopkins and Rebecca's mother in a very different light.

Could it be that the witch-hunt sparked by tailor Rivet's concern for his wife gave Hopkins the chance to dispose of a personal problem that was becoming troublesome? Was 'the old beldam West' as Hopkins called her, the real target? Hopkins, Stearne and four women who helped in the witch-hunt all described Anne West as an 'old beldam' in statements delivered on the same day. But the examination of Elizabeth Clarke painted a very different picture of the widow from Lawford. She said West 'seemed much to pity her for her lameness (having but one leg) and her poverty.' Anne West was certainly poor and she had a bad name, but she did not lack strength of character or, it seems, some feelings of charity and sympathy for a crippled old woman. One might think that an old woman with such a handicap would have been the object of Christian charity from the likes of Hopkins and Stearne, but Puritans could be less than charitable. They often railed against the indiscriminate giving of charity declaring that it resulted in paupers refusing to face up to their responsibilities; it encouraged them in their indolence, and it robbed them of discipline to God and society. Perhaps Stearne's animosity toward Anne West was caused by the fact that she held to a brand of the Christian religion very different to his own. Hopkins may well have recognised this and made use of it as he orchestrated the witch-hunt for his own ends.

According to her daughter's first confession, Anne West had 'desired of her spirit that she might be freed from all her enemies and have no trouble', hardly malicious sentiments. It was later, under pressure from Hopkins and Edes, that Rebecca declared that her mother had been guilty of maleficia.

Perhaps the most curious feature of Rebecca West's involvement in the affair is that she escaped scot-free. She confessed to bewitching her neighbours and having a long-term sexual relationship with the Devil – in the eyes of any Puritan that was witchery of the worst kind and deserving of death. In Stearne's words, 'This young woman confessed the naming of their imps, and the manner, which I am ashamed to express; and the initiation of a witch, and every particular thing at large, especially she confessed how the devil took her by the hand, and the manner and words were used at her marriage when she was married to the devil (as she confessed): a fearful thing to declare.' Like the five women she had named as witches, she was charged with keeping familiars and bewitching, but they were hanged and she was not. The charges against the two Clarkes, Anne Leech and Elizabeth Gooding were endorsed by Hopkins and Stearne but not those against the Wests. Indeed there is no record of a plea or verdict in Rebecca's case. Was it intended from the start that Rebecca should escape the noose?

Strings were certainly pulled. When it was all over Stearne complained about an unnamed man who was 'one of the greatest agents in Colchester business'. He wrote, 'I saw him labour and endeavour all he could to keep this woman whom he so much held withal from her legal trial, and likewise heard him threaten both me and all that had given evidence against her, or informed what manner of woman she had been in her life and conversation, to their knowledge, or as they had heard: yes, as I since have heard she was condemned at that assize and by his procurement reprieved. Since which time, on her behalf, this has been done.'

Anne West was tried at Chelmsford in July 1645, found guilty and hanged at Manningtree with three of her friends whereas her daughter Rebecca disappears from history. Anne West consistently denied the witchcraft charges against her, so could it be that as far as Hopkins was concerned her real crime was that she was a mother concerned for a daughter who had granted sexual favours in return for promises by 'a proper young man' who had no intention of honouring them. Had sweet words and false promises turned Rebecca's head? Would she have been so eager to escape her situation that she would agree to make such a dangerous confession knowing that it could mean the sacrifice of her own and her mother's life? And could Hopkins have been that man? With the mother dead, who would credit any claims against him by a young woman who was a self-confessed witch? And by the time Rebecca was free again it was high summer and Hopkins was on his meteoric rise to celebrity status.

This suggestion may, on first consideration, be considered outrageous, but certainly it is not beyond the bounds of credibility. Stranger things have happened and as events soon demonstrated, Hopkins was a remarkably ruthless man. And as his witch-hunt gathered pace and spread across several counties, criticism of the man and his methods emerged with claims that there was more than a little hypocrisy about Hopkins and his 'crusade'.

Now to return to Friday March 21, 1645, the day the magistrates, Sir Thomas Bowes and Sir Harbottle Grimston, listened to the statement by John Rivet and the confession by Rebecca West. Horrified by what they heard, the two magistrates immediately authorised old Elizabeth Clarke to be subjected to the interrogation technique known as 'watching and keeping'. Hopkins said it was intended to force a witch to call her imps into open view. Stearne declared, '....watching has produced true and strange effects, and is a great means (under God) to bring them [witches] to confession.'

After three days and four nights, and in the presence of as many as ten witnesses, old Elizabeth Clarke at last gave the witch-hunters the confession they wanted. Hopkins claimed that after she had admitted having 'carnal copulation' with the Devil for six or seven years, she made her imps appear. One called Jarmara was in the form of a fat white dog with short legs; one called Vinegar Tom was like a greyhound; another called Newes was like a polecat with a big head, and there was one in the form of a black rabbit named Sack and Sugar which was intent on harming Master Stearne. Hopkins later elaborated on what Vinegar Tom looked like by describing him as 'a long-legged greyhound, with a head like an ox, with a long tail and broad eyes [which] transformed himself into the shape of a child of four years old without a head, and gave half a dozen turns about the house and vanished at the door'.

Hopkins went on to claim that as he made his way home later that night from Richard Edwards' house his dog was injured when they encountered two imps in the shape of a white kitten and a large black cat. Stearne's declaration was similar to Hopkins' though he did add that the imp called Sack and Sugar had intended to get in his throat and give him 'a feast of toads in his belly'.

Stearne later wrote another account of the encounter. After stating that he was 'one which caused her to be questioned', he described what happened when he and Hopkins went to get the names of Clarke's fellow witches during the 'watching'. 'She said to us, if you will stay I will show you my imps for they be ready to come. Then said Mr Hopkin, Bess will they do us no harm? No said she, what?

Did you think I am afraid of my children?' Then she called in her imps which, curiously, the witnesses saw in different forms. She told Hopkins that she regularly had sex with the Devil who came to her in the likeness of a 'tall proper [handsome] black haired gentleman, a properer man than yourself'.

Elizabeth Clarke was 'watched' until midnight and then she was allowed some sleep. The next day, Tuesday March 25, was Lady Day and in the old way of reckoning it was the first day of the new year. So on the first day on 1645, Hopkins and Stearne described what had happened the previous night, and then seven more witnesses 'laid information' before the magistrates. They declared that Clarke had told them that in recent weeks Anne West had been responsible for bewitching several people to death, and that two and a half years previously she had raised a wind to sink a ship thus causing a brother of one of the witnesses to be drowned. Clarke was brought before the magistrates and she said that Anne West had sent her two imps, one of which 'would help her to a husband who should maintain her ever after'.

Warrants were issued for the arrest of Anne West and the three other women named by Rebecca West. They were soon rounded up, searched and then 'watched', and by the end of April the magistrates had plenty more confessions and witness statements placed in front of them detailing the devilish deeds of the four women.

Robert Taylor, a shopkeeper in Manningtree, said that Elizabeth Gooding [or Goodwin] had killed his horse by witchcraft by making its belly rumble like a 'foul chimney on fire'. Describing Gooding as 'a lewd woman', he added that she had done it after he had refused to let her have half a pound of cheese on credit. Gooding denied everything he said.

Helen Clarke was said to have had an argument with Mary, the wife of Edward Parsley, and she had taken her revenge by causing their daughter to sicken and die. Clarke denied killing anyone but admitted that she had kept an imp called Elimanzer in the shape of a white dog which she fed on milk-pottage.

Anne Leech said that with Gooding and Clarke she had sent imps to kill cows belonging to Richard Edwards. She also admitted sending her imps to kill people and animals over thirty years. Her confession obviously refreshed Richard Edwards' memory because he then came forward and said that about a year previously he had been driving his cows past Anne Leech's house one Sunday when a black one had collapsed and died. And the next day the same thing had happened to a white cow. He also believed that she and Gooding had caused the death of his infant son. And with his memory stirred by Rebecca West's confession, Richard Edwards also recalled how three months before he had almost been thrown from his horse when it had been frightened by an imp shrieking like a polecat. Then Prudence Hart of Lawford stepped forward, her memory jogged by the confession of young Rebecca West. She told the magistrates that she had been taken lame when something fell onto her bed one night and later she had suffered a miscarriage, all of which she blamed on Anne and Rebecca West.

During April and May 1645 there were more accusations, more body searches and more confessions as the Manningtree witch-hunt gathered pace and its poison spread into nearby towns and villages. Bad feeling caused by old feuds and old animosities, often between women, resulted in more women from Tendring Hundred being locked up in Colchester Castle. Often a charge of witchcraft arose from a trivial incident, or simply from having a bad reputation, or both. Susan Sparrow claimed that thirty years before, while sharing a house with Mary Greenleaf, a woman of 'ill name', she had heard imps being suckled under the bedclothes and noticed that a leveret sometimes came and sat by the door. 'But whether this was an imp in the shape of a leveret or had any relation to Mary Greenleaf, she knows not, but does confess she wondered very much to see a leveret, wild by nature, to come so frequently and sit openly before the door in such a familiar way.' Two women who searched Mary, a woman of more than 60 years from Alresford, swore she 'had biggs or teats in her secret parts and they verily believe these teats are suckled by her imps.' Greenleaf said she did not know she had such teats until she was told about them after the search and her explanation was that she must have been born with them.

Elizabeth Otley from Wivenhoe claimed that Mary Johnson carried in her pocket an imp like a rat without ears or tail, and one day she had pushed it through a hole in her front door and made it rock her child's cradle. On another occasion when she came to the house, Johnson gave the child an apple and a kiss 'and soon after the child sickened and died.' This was gossip spread by another Wivenhoe woman, Alice Dixon, who was also suspected of witchery. Johnson denied having anything to do with the death of the Otley child and said it was Alice Dixon who 'did the mischief.' Elizabeth Otley's woes had not ended there because she then suffered 'extreme pains in her body' during which times Mary Johnson came to her house pleading that she had not caused the child's death. Otley decided to end her pains by having some of Mary Johnson's blood so when they next met there was a scuffle in which she made Johnson's teeth bleed. 'Immediately after her extraordinary pains left her and her stomach [appetite] came to her, she having eaten little or nothing a fortnight before, and slept very well the night following having been restless by reason of her extreme pain.'

Mary Johnson had another enemy in Wivenhoe. One day she had met George Durrant's wife Annabel leading her child by the hand toward Fingringhoe. Johnson stopped, stroked the child and gave it a piece of bread and butter. Within a quarter of an hour the child was lame and shrieking its head off, so much so that it had to be carried home and eight days later it was dead. Then things had got worse for Annabel and her husband. 'Immediately after the death of her child she was taken with extreme pains in her body, sometimes every day or at least every third day, for the space of seven or eight months together, as if she had been to be delivered of a child, but was not with child. Setting up of broom in an out-house presently after her child was dead she had the perfect representation of a shape, to her thinking, like Mary Johnson, and was struck with a lameness in her arms and such a stiffness that three or four that came to help her were not able to bow her arms and she continued speechless all that day and the night following and had such a weakness in the rest of her limbs that she was carried into her house by some of her friends and continued for the space of a fortnight.

'She being charged by the constable by virtue of a warrant to give information before the Justices against Mary Johnson this day [April 29] her husband called her up in the morning, wishing her to make ready to go before the Justices, and presently he gave a great shriek and said Mary Johnson would be his death and had a great swelling risen up in his breast, and now lies sweating and in great extremity. And at this very instant a noise was heard in the room where her husband lay like a hornet, and thereupon her husband cried out 'It comes, it comes, now goodwife Johnson's imp is come, now she has my life' and forthwith a great part of the wall in the room fell down. This informant verily believes that Mary Johnson was the cause of her child's death and is now the cause of her husband's extremity.'

Joseph Long, the minister at Great Clacton, claimed that Anne Cooper had told him that she had three black imps called Wynowe, Jeso and Panu and that she had given another one called Tomboy to her daughter. As for bewitching to death, she admitted sending an imp to kill a girl in Clacton ten years earlier as well as having cursed a horse which broke its neck. When the reverend gentlemen told Elizabeth Hare, another woman from Clacton, that she was accused of having imps 'she praying to God with her hands upwards, that if she were guilty of any such thing He would show some example upon her, presently after she shook and quivered and fell down to the ground backward, and tumbled up and down upon the ground and has continued sick ever since.'

Margaret Moone, a widow from Thorpe-le-Soken, was suspected because she was 'a woman of a very bad fame'. It was reported that something like a rat had dropped from beneath her skirts just before the room was invaded by 'an extreme offensive stink' which the watchers could scarcely endure. They said that she confessed to having twelve imps but could not remember their names. She also admitted bewitching people, killing children and animals, spoiling beer brewings and ruining batches of bread.

The catalogue of crimes piled up against Margaret Moone. Another instance of her witchery, so they said, was the occasion when she was turned out of her house because another family could pay more rent. Strangely, however, the new tenants did not prosper in the house and although the wife kept the house clean and tidy her clothes were so thick with lice that they could be scraped off with a stick.

The next stage of Margaret Moone's ordeal was to be searched for secret teats. Hopkins' associates Mary Philips and Frances Mills were sent for and they duly found the incriminating teats in Moone's 'secret parts'. One searcher claimed the teats 'seemed to have been lately suckled and they were not like piles because she knows well what they are, having been troubled with them herself.' Moone offered to entice her imps into the room with some bread and beer but when nothing came through the hole in the wall she said her 'devilish daughters had carried her imps away in a white bag.' So her daughters were also searched and found to have teats in their privy parts as well. Margaret Moone did have one small measure of satisfaction against Mills and Philips, the 'Manningtree rogues' as she called them. As they were crossing a footbridge on their way to Thorpe to conduct the search Philips had felt a smack on the back of her head and been knocked into a ditch up to her neck.

The number of round-ups and searches multiplied as the witch-mania spread. One was in the village of Ramsey where Elizabeth Harvey and Mariana Hockett, both widows, and Sarah Hating were taken into custody. Again Mary Philips helped with the body searches and incriminating teats were found on Hating and Harvey but not on Hockett. The reason they found no marks on Hockett was revealed by her sister, Sarah Barton, who was being held in prison in Harwich on suspicion of witchcraft. She said her sister had taken precautions against just such a search and 'had cut off her biggs whereby she might have been the more suspected to have been a witch, and laid plasters to those places.' According to her treacherous sister, Hockett's imps were called Littleman, Prettyman and Dainty.

Francis Stock, once the village constable at Ramsey, said that when he had gone to impress Sarah Hating's husband into the army she had shouted threats at him and soon after a snake had been found in his house. Then his wife had been taken sick and died, as did his two children.

Five women from St Osyth were accused of witchcraft. Rose Hallybread, a widow of more than sixty years, was said to have bewitched Robert Turner's servant so that the unfortunate man crowed like a cock, barked like a dog, groaned violently and struggled so much that four or five strong men could not hold him down. On top of that he sometimes sang songs without moving his lips.

Hallybread confessed that she had been given an imp by Goodwife Hagtree fifteen years previously. She had fed it on oatmeal, suckled it and then lost it. She went on to admit bewitching a boy to death by putting an imp like a grey bird in a cranny of the door. She added that she and three friends, Susan Cock, Margaret Landish and Joyce Boanes [or Boones], were responsible for the barking and crowing by Turner's manservant, having sent their four imps after him because he had refused to give them some firewood. Boanes said her imps had killed sheep and lambs over the years and as far as the singing servant was concerned her imp made him bark, Hallybread's made him sing, Cock's made him crow and Landish's made him groan.

Susan Cock declared that when her mother was on her deathbed she had been given two imps, a mouse called Susan and a yellow cat called Bess. She confessed that the four women had killed sheep belonging to John Spalls because his wife had refused to let her have some curds when she was pregnant. With Landish's aid she had killed some hogs owned by Thomas Mannock and 'the occasion of the offence was because Mannock's wife refused to give her such relief as she desired, telling her that she was a young woman and able to work for her living.'

The fifth woman from St Osyth to be accused of witchery was widow Rebecca Jones who said the first time she met the Devil was when he knocked on her door in the guise of a 'very handsome young man.' She had met him again when going to St Osyth to sell butter but then he was in a ragged suit and he gave her three imps like moles saying they 'would avenge her on her enemies and bid her murder some, but not too many.' She said that she and Joyce Boanes had sent imps to kill Thomas Bumstead and his wife because they had beaten her son when he ate their honey. Joan Cooper, a widow from Great Holland, told the magistrates that she had been a witch for twenty years using two mouse-like imps called Jack and Prickear, and one like a frog called Frog. Anne Cate [or Cade, alias Anne Maidenhead] was from the same village and she declared that she also had an imp like a mouse called Prickear. She also had an imp like a sparrow called Sparrow which killed people for her. She had sent Sparrow to kill a child because its mother had refused her a pint of milk, and a man's wife because she would not repay the two pence she owed.

The result of the witch-hunt that had started in Manningtree in March was a mass trial of witches at Chelmsford in July. Never before had so many women been arraigned at the same time on charges of witchcraft. The St Osyth witch trial in 1582 had involved thirteen defendants and the Pendle trials of 1612 had concerned nineteen. The records are incomplete but it appears that some thirty-seven women were charged and at least 17 of them were hanged. Hopkins said twenty-nine were condemned with four of them being brought back to Manningtree to be hanged. He says their crime had been to send 'the Devil like a Bear to kill him in his garden'. Some of the others were pardoned or reprieved, and it seems that as many as eleven died in jail either before or after coming to trial. The fate of some of them, including Rebecca West, is unknown.

The accused women and their likely fates were –
Sarah Barton of Ramsey, fate unknown.
Helen Bretton of Kirby, hanged.
Sarah Bright, a widow of Manningtree, hanged.
Joyce Boones [Boanes] of St Osyth, hanged.
Dorothy Brooke acquitted but remanded in gaol.
Anne Cate [Cade] of Great Holland, hanged.
Elizabeth Clarke of Manningtree, hanged.
Helen Clarke of Manningtree, hanged.
Susan Cocke of St Osyth, condemned, pardoned, died in gaol.
Mary Cooke, a widow of Langham, died in gaol.

Anne Cooper of Great Clacton, hanged.

Joan Cooper, a widow of Great Holland, died in gaol.

Mary Coppin of Kirby Le Soken condemned, reprieved, died in gaol.

Alice Dixon, a widow of Wivenhoe, hanged.

Elizabeth Gibson of Thorpe-le-Soken, died in gaol.

Elizabeth Gooding [Goodwin] of Manningtree, hanged.

Mary Greenleaf, a widow of Alresford, acquitted but died in gaol.

Margaret [Margery] Grewe of Walton-le-Soken [Walton on the Naze], hanged.

Rose Hallybread of St Osyth, died in gaol.

Elizabeth Hare of Great Clacton, hanged.

Elizabeth Harvey of Ramsey, condemned, reprieved, died in gaol.

Sarah Hating of Ramsey, hanged.

Marian Hockett, a widow of Ramsey, hanged.

Mary Johnson of Wivenhoe, condemned, reprieved, held in prison.

Rebecca Jones, a widow of St Osyth, probably hanged.

Margaret Landish of St Osyth, hanged.

Anne Leech, a widow of Mistley, hanged.

Bridget Mayers of Holland, condemned, reprieved, probably died in gaol.

Margaret Moone, a widow of Thorpe-le-Soken, condemned, said to have died on way to execution.

Joan Rowle [Rowley], a widow of Leigh, acquitted but remanded in custody.

Mary Starling of Langham, condemned but repreived.

Anne Thurston of Great Clacton, condemned, reprieved, remanded in gaol.

Dorothy Waters of Great Clacton, condemned, reprieved, died in gaol.

Susanna Went, a widow of Langham, condemned but repreived, perhaps died in gaol.

Anne West, a widow of Lawford, hanged.

Rebecca West, daughter of Anne West, of Lawford, indicted, verdict not known, one report states that she was acquitted, fate unknown.

Mary Wiles, a widow of Great Clacton, hanged.

The numbers involved was not the only sensational feature. The trials were unusual because they were presided over not by a judge but by Robert Rich, Earl of Warwick, the man Parliament had appointed to command the fleet. Not only was Rich a lord with strong Puritan beliefs, but he was a cousin to Robert Devereux, Earl of Essex, whose marriage to Frances Howard had ended so scandalously with talk of him being bewitched into impotency.

Framlingham Mere with the town's ancient castle in the background. It was here that the notorious witch-hunter Matthew Hopkins used the swimming test on many of his victims in the summer of 1645. One of those subjected to the test was an old clergyman from a nearby village.

An Abundance of Sad Confessions

The Manningtree witch-hunt was the making of Matthew Hopkins. Almost overnight he went from being a middling sized fish in a very small pond to a celebrity [or villain] on the national stage. It's usually only the super-famous [Shakespeare, William the Conqueror, Princess Diana], the 'super-heroes' [Nelson, Hereward the Wake, Florence Nightingale] and the villains, outlaws and sometimes the murderers [Robin Hood, Dick Turpin, Jack the Ripper] whose names are readily preserved in the national memory. The judgement of history has been that Hopkins was a villain, but to many people at the start of his witch-hunting activities he was certainly more a hero than a villain. Perceptions can change very rapidly and it seems that in the eyes of many people that Hopkins went from hero to villain very rapidly. And as in the case of many opportunists like him we do not know very much about him until he suddenly burst on the scene as a self-appointed witch-hunter.

Hopkins was born in 1620, the fourth of six children. His father, the Rev. James Hopkins, was the parson of Great Wenham, a small village some six miles to the south-west of Ipswich. As a priest's son Matthew would have received a better education than most boys. It appears that he then tried to make his way in business in Ipswich but the venture whatever it was failed and he became a clerk working in the small Stour estuary ports of Mistley and nearby Manningtree. There he seems to have made an adequate living though perhaps he harboured a smouldering resentment born from a conviction that his status was less than he deserved. His closest associate in the witch-hunts was John Stearne, a religious fanatic who described him as 'the son of a godly minister', so it was natural that Hopkins should take a leading role in the Puritan pro-Parliament clique that governed Manningtree's society. He also made himself known to the local magistrates. By the time circumstances conspired to offer them the opportunity for a witch-hunt Hopkins and Stearne had developed an impressive network of local relationships – business, religious, legal and personal – upon which they could call for backing. The Manningtree witch-hunt could never have happened without a high degree of active local support.

To some writers Hopkins was an 'unmitigated scoundrel', 'a cruel bigot' and 'not only an impostor but a veritable inhuman monster of cruelty'. The truth is none of these. Matthew Hopkins was the right man for the job who happened to be in the right place at the right time. Yes, he was ruthless and ambitious, and somewhat resentful, and when the witch-hunt suddenly and unexpectedly developed a momentum of its own, he seized the opportunity to exercise power and win the praise of like-minded men. With his confidence bolstered by religious conviction and the arrogant certainties of youth – he was in his mid 20s – Hopkins found himself suddenly riding high on a popular wave of power and adulation. As well as being a high road to power and fame, it also proved to be a road to some profit.

Such was his sudden and meteoric rise to power and prominence that one of his critics said in despair 'people talk more passionately of the infallible and wonderful power of the witch-finders than they do of God, Christ or the gospel.' He went on, 'Every accident of nature is attributed to an effect of witchcraft, for this a witch must be sought out and a witch searcher summoned.' New-found power, praise and profit like that would turn any young man's head.

The arrest of almost forty witches in one corner of Essex in only a few weeks struck some people with wonder, some with terror and a few with disgust. People were amazed and fearful that witchery was so rife because if all that they heard were true the country must be overrun by witches and their imps. Others muttered that this witch-finder was just a bully in high boots and in time people began to say he was fleecing the country and living like a lord while labourers toiled in the fields for six pence a day. Certainly after his death the prevalent view was that he had been in the 'trade' for the money.

James Howell, the royalist writer, traveller, diplomat and for eight years a prisoner of Roundheads, wrote early in 1646 that there were 'multitudes of witches among us' and that above two hundred witches had been indicted in Essex and Suffolk and more than half of them hanged. His view was that Puritan iconoclasm was at fault. 'God guard us from the Devil, for I think he was never so busy upon any part of the Earth that was enlightened with the beams of Christianity; nor do I wonder at it for there is never a cross left to fright him away.' The trials of the witches from in and around Manningtree were held at Chelmsford at the end of July but Hopkins, Stearne and their searcher-in-chief, Mary Phillips, did not wait around for the law to take its course. They rode into Suffolk eager to find more witches and their diligence was instantly rewarded. Soon scores of frightened women and a few men were being held in jail. Parliament granted a special commission of Oyer and Terminer to oversee the Suffolk witch-hunt with serjeant-at-law John Godbolt, two Puritan priests of radical opinion, Edmund Calamy and Samuel Fairclough, and local magistrates appointed to conduct the trials. Godbolt, Calamy and Fairclough all had local links. Judge Godbolt was MP for Bury St Edmunds while Edmund Calamy the elder was a Cambridge-educated anti-royalist of Presbyterian persuasion who had been vicar at Swaffham Prior near Cambridge and lecturer at Bury St Edmunds where he got into trouble over religious observances. He was one of the five authors of *Smectymnuus*, a rejection of Bishop of Norwich Joseph Hall's plea for moderate episcopacy and church ritual. One commentator said their work 'was stuffed with malice, spleen and rascally invectives'. [*Smectymnuus* comes from the initials of the five men – Stephen Marshall, Edmund Calamy, Thomas Young, Matthew Newcomen and William [uu] Spurstow]. The Smec five – all educated in the religious hothouse atmosphere of Cambridge – had strong links with East Anglia and, indeed, with towns and villages not many miles from Hopkins' boyhood home of Great Wenham, or Manningtree. Marshall had been vicar of Finchingfield in the 1630s where it was said, 'He governs the conscience of all the rich Puritans in those parts and in many places far remote'. He was disciplined 'for want of conformity' and when the Civil War began he preached to the Parliamentary troops on the eve of the Battle of Edge Hill. Young was Master of Jesus College and sometime vicar at Stowmarket and

Newcomen, who was related to Calamy by marriage, had been lecturer at Dedham where he had succeeded 'Roaring' John Rogers whose enthusiastic preaching often filled the church to overflowing. Another influential member of the commission appointed by Parliament to oversee the witch-hunt was Haverhill-born Samuel Fairclough, a 50-year-old Cambridge educated priest who had been in trouble with the Bishop of Norwich because of his radical ways. In 1629 Suffolk's leading Puritan magnate, Sir Nathaniel Barnardiston, had offered him the living at Kedington, a position Fairclough held for 25 years. Stearne certainly did not consider Fairclough to be very radical because he described as 'an able orthodox divine'. Indeed, during the Suffolk witch-hunt Fairclough was close at hand to become involved in one of the cases uncovered by Stearne. A woman by the name of Binkes from Haverhill admitted to suckling an invisible imp and when she was questioned by Stearne she confessed that a fly that was buzzing around the room was one of her imps too. She asked to see Fairclough and when he came she immediately denied everything she had confessed saying that if she were a witch God should make an example of her and make her imps appear. Stearne claimed that the fly-imp was then seen 'fastened upon another place of her body....and so remained above quarter of an hour....she only crying out to have it pulled off.' Eventually some frightened women wiped the fly away with a cloth and 'what became of it after they knew not'. Binkes continued to deny everything and was acquitted although Stearne asked, 'Was this woman fitting to live, this evidence, with others, being [brought] against her by credible witnesses?'

Faced with such an unprecedented number of prisoners flowing into the county's jails, and a growing unease with the witch-finders' methods, the commission put a stop to Hopkins and Stearne using the swimming and watching techniques. One report of the time sounded a note of caution to the witch-hunters by observing that the commission was charged 'that a most special care should be taken both in the execution of the law and also that all tenderness might be used in a matter wherein the lives and immortal souls of so many are concerned.'

When eventually the criticism of his methods could no longer be ignored, Hopkins' angry response was to issue a hastily written pamphlet called *The Discovery of Witches*. The tone is that of a blustering bully who seeks to shift the blame onto others – onto 'able Divines whom I reverence'; onto judges and magistrates, witnesses and searchers, and even onto the witches themselves, and, of course, he blames the false promises of the Devil. Sometimes he answers arrogantly and always he angrily denies any deliberate wrongdoing. If he had indeed 'met with the Devil and cheated him of his book wherein were written the names of all the witches in England' it was surely 'to his great commendation and no disgrace at all.' His skill as a witch-finder came not 'from his profound learning or from much reading of learned authors concerning that subject' but from experience 'which though it be meanly esteemed of' was the 'surest and safest way to judge by'. The experience he had gained, he said, could be acquired by anyone.

He admits that suspects were swum but says that King James's book justified it, and as for those kept awake or made to walk until their feet were blistered, that was the result of their 'own stubborn will' or the fault of their imps. He pleads that he 'is of a better conscience' than to allow torture, and, anyway, confessions gained by such methods he would 'account of no validity'. These are lies.

He says it was for magistrates to examine the accused with 'much care and diligence' and claims that it was his desire 'that all magistrates and jurors would a little more than ever they did, examine witnesses about the interrogated confessions'. As for fleecing the country of money he pleads that he only went to places which sent for him and where people were glad to see him. And, so he claims, his fee was only twenty shillings per town no matter how many witches he found. Hopkins was paid £23 by Stowmarket, £15 by King's Lynn and he made three visits to Aldeburgh earning a total of £6.

The fact that he felt compelled to write it shows that the self-appointed saviour had become a man despised by many. The majority of his victims were the poorest and weakest people in society just as

Reginald Scot had described them over half a century earlier. Then, in a plea for charity instead of intolerance, Scot had written, 'For God knows many of these poor wretches had more need to be relieved than chastised; and more meet [proper] were a preacher to admonish them than a jailer to keep them; and a physician more necessary to help them than an executioner or tormentor to hang or burn them.' It was an aspiration wasted on Hopkins.

Some fifty years later when the belief in witchcraft was fast becoming unsustainable, Richard Baxter tried to stem the tide of doubt with a book called *The Certainty of the World of Spirits*. He wrote, 'The hanging of a great number of witches in Suffolk and Essex by the discovery of one Hopkins in 1645 and 1646 is famously known. Mr Calamy went along with the judges in the circuit to hear their confessions and see that there were no fraud or wrong done them. Abundance of sad confessions were made by them; by which some testified that there are certain punishments which they were to undergo if they did not some hurt as was appointed them.'

Certainly there was an abundance of sad confessions. There was also an abundance of fraud and wrongdoing. Hopkins and Stearne parted company soon after arriving in Suffolk with Stearne concentrating his efforts in the south-west of the county around Sudbury while Hopkins took horse for the north-eastern area around Framlingham and along the coast. Stearne usually used the body search for witches' marks while Hopkins used a combination of searching, watching and, perhaps for the first time at Framlingham, the swimming test. Their interrogations concentrated on gaining confessions of pacts with the Devil, details of their sexual activities and the suckling of imps. There were more tales of arguments being quickly followed by disasters and of the Devil falsely promising to alleviate the poverty of old women. Anne Moats of Framlingham said her imps killed cattle and the Devil appeared 'after she had been cursing her husband and her children.' Shoemaker John Spink claimed that seven years previously Elizabeth Fillet of Wetherden had cursed his workshop with a troublesome rat and mole after an argument over shoe repairs. At Playford the miller had threatened to throw Margaret Legat into the river if she called at his house again after his child suffered an illness which baffled the doctor from Ipswich but which the child said was caused by wasp stings. Thomas Hudson said he went lame after 'a falling out with oaths' with Anne Ellis of Mettingham but he 'did now begin to mend' after changing his doctor. Fillet, Legat and Ellis were all cleared, but Moats' fate is uncertain.

Margaret Bennet of Bacton said she had made love with the Devil when he took her into a thicket of bushes. She had sent her imp to make a cow kick the woman who had refused her some butter. Her neighbour, widow Mary Bush, admitted bewitching cows and turkeys and said the Devil had been coming into her bed two or three times a week for fifteen years to have the use of her body but he 'was colder than man and heavier and could not perform nature as man.' Anne Hammer of Creeting had a similar experience. After agreeing to 'free her of hell torments' and promising that she would never want for anything, the Devil would come to her through the keyhole in the likeness of a black man 'and have the use of her body but was heavier and colder, and lay all over her as a man and used not to speak but only to ask to lie with her and as she thought performed nature'.

One of Anne Hammer's imps was a mole while Elizabeth Richmond from Bramford had familiars in the form of a dog with cloven feet and a hog called Jack, and during the course of the witch-hunts the range of imps increased remarkably. As well as the usual cats, dogs, moles and mice, Hopkins' victims confessed to having imps in the form of blackbirds, crows, toads, rats, crabs, polecats, squirrels, chickens, turkeys and even flies, grasshoppers and spiders.

As the numbers of those detained increased so Hopkins became more ruthless and arrogant in his behaviour and more convinced that he was above challenge. A Suffolk parson who spoke out against him from his pulpit was forced to recant his objection and another old parson was one of those who suffered blatant injustice at Hopkins' hands.

Brandeston Church, like many other village churches, displays a list of its vicars from previous centuries but in one respect Brandeston's roll is unique. Beginning with Roger de Hecham in 1308, it shows that in 1596 George Lowes was succeeded by John Lowes and that he held the position for almost fifty years. But it is not the length of his incumbency that makes John Lowes noteworthy but the words printed beside his name – 'hanged as witch.'

As the spring of 1645 turned into summer, John Lowes was eighty years old and entering his fiftieth year as vicar of the small Suffolk village and when Hopkins descended on the nearby small market town of Framlingham some of the old man's parishioners saw it as a chance to be rid of him.

Lowes' years in Brandeston had been punctuated by outbursts of anger and enmity. Many of his flock detested him and for years they had been trying to have him removed. They described him as 'vexatious' and 'of turbulent spirit' and they objected to the 'strange points of doctrine' which he expounded from the pulpit on Sundays. Parson and those parishioners of Puritan persuasion had been involved in a vendetta of charge and counter-charge until accusations of slander, witchcraft and disturbing the peace were made against each other. On one occasion Lowes gave one of his flock a bloody nose during an argument in the churchyard and tempers had run high when he took the side of a woman from the village who had been accused of witchery. She was arraigned and condemned and then Lowes himself faced a similar charge but was cleared.

His enemies regularly petitioned the Church authorities to have him removed but without success. Lowes was certainly an irascible, argumentative, and humorless man who was ever willing to slap a lawsuit on a parishioner who crossed him in a minor dispute. He and a fellow vicar from a nearby parish were even the subjects of a pamphlet headlined *A Magazine of Scandal* which was published anonymously but was almost certainly the work of their enemies. These old quarrels, religious antagonisms and his reputation of being a witch made John Lowes an obvious target for the attention of the witch-finder. Hopkins extracted confessions linking Lowes with two suspected women witches from Framlingham and the old vicar was seized and subjected to the ordeal of 'swimming' in the waters of the mere beneath the walls of Framlingham's ancient castle. Then he was 'watched' night and day until 'he was weary of his life'. It was all too much for the old man and he told his tormentors what they wanted to hear. He admitted having imps which, he said, forced him to 'employ them about some evil actions' like killing cattle and sinking a ship.

It was said that Lowes was at Landguard Ford near Felixstowe one day when he saw a flotilla of ships. 'One of his three imps, namely his yellow one appeared and asked him what he should do and he bade it go and sink a ship and showed the imp a new ship amongst the middle of the rest, one that belonged to Ipswich. The imp went forthwith away and he stood and viewed the ships on the sea as they were sailing and perceived that ship immediately to be in more trouble and danger than the rest for he said the water was more boisterous near that [ship] than the rest, tumbling up and down with waves, as if water had been boiled in a pot and soon after in a short time it sank directly down into the sea as he stood and viewed it when all the rest sailed away in safety. There he confessed he made fourteen widows in one quarter of an hour.' Years later Bishop Francis Hutchinson said the story of the sinking ship was 'a monstrous tale without any tolerable proof to support it.' But the special court that tried Lowes at Bury St Edmunds in August 1645 accepted the story without bothering to find out if in fact such a ship had sunk. With his mind recovered from the delirium of exhaustion, Lowes resolutely maintained his innocence in court but his pleas were disregarded and he was hanged with sixteen women and another man. The story goes that 'being precluded Christian burial from the nature of his offence, he composedly and in an audible voice read the service over himself on the way to execution.'

On the eve of their executions, the condemned men and women decided to make a last show of defiance. They agreed amongst themselves not to admit their guilt on the gallows as was the custom. Stearne states that their refusal to show any penitence caused them to die 'very desperately', except for the woman who revealed their plan. Years later Bishop Hutchinson wrote to the vicar of Brandeston about the Lowes case and his letter was passed on to Mr Revett, the village squire whose family had lived at Brandeston Hall for generations.

Church and hall still stand close to each other, the former still with several memorials to members of the Revett family and the latter now used as a school.

Squire Revett replied, 'In answer to your request concerning Mr Lowes, my father was always of the opinion that Mr Lowes suffered wrongfully, and has often said that he did believe he was no more a wizard than he was. I have heard it from them that watched with him, that they kept him awake several nights together, and ran him backwards and forwards about the room until he was out of breath. Then they rested him a little and then ran him again: and thus they did for several days and nights together, till he was weary of his life and was scarce sensible of what he said or did. They swam him at Framlingham, but it was no true rule to try him by; for they put in honest people at the same time and they swam as well as he.'

They also 'swam' Margery With alias Chinery. She was interrogated by Hopkins until she confessed to causing a child to die of fits and blue spots, then adding that Lowes had urged her to 'never confess any thing about witchcraft.'

Lowes was hanged with four people from Halesworth among whom were a husband and wife, four women from Copdock and two from Chattisham. Thomas Everard, a Halesworth barrelmaker, said he had met the Devil in the form of a noiseless black dog which had jumped out in front of him. This sounds suspiciously like a retelling of the old East Anglian folktale of the phantom dog Black Shuck. Everard's wife Mary said they had bewitched the town beer supply. Copdock widow Mary Skipper said that when her husband died the Devil persuaded her to become a witch by promising to pay her debts and ensure 'she should never want.' Mary Bacon and Anne Alderman of Chattisham said their imps, a grasshopper and a squirrel, came from an old neighbour called Mother Cotnell who may well have been hanged too.

Mary Smith of Glemham admitted selling some imps. Margery Sparham of Mendham, who was described as a lewd woman who seldom went to church, admitted having blackbirds as her familiars. The old idea invented by Sprenger and Kramer that priests could not be bewitched surfaced in the case of Katherine Tooley of Westleton who admitted having angry words with the village parson one day and sending her imp called Jackly after him. But the imp returned saying that he had failed in his mission to harm the parson because 'he served God'. [The parson happened to be one of the witnesses against her.] At Westleton there is an old tradition that dancing around the so-called witch's stone in the churchyard will summon the Devil. A few miles away at Dunwich lived an old pauper called Mother Collitt. She was kept awake for three days and nights before confessing that the Devil had tempted her to kill her children because otherwise she would 'always continue poor'. He pledged to give her money but never did. Mother Collitt had been implicated by Elizabeth Southern who also came from Dunwich. She said that the two of them had had an argument with the result that Collitt had sent the Devil after her in the form of a crab which came and nipped her while she was in bed. Southern added that the Devil had promised to give her 2s 6d but had failed to pay her blaming 'the hardness of the times'.

One of the small minority of men accused of witchcraft was John Bysack of Great Waldingfield. He said the Devil came through his window in the shape of a sandy coloured dog. He said his imps were snails and one killed cows, another killed hogs, another sheep, another horses, another fowls and the last one killed Christians. Another man, Nicholas Hempstead of Creeting confessed to killing some horses in Cromwell's army because the constables forced him to do military service.

Again there were episodes of young women confessing that they had been drawn into witchcraft by their parents. The witch-hunters' youngest victim was a nine year old boy from Rattlesden, a village where Stearne detected a gang of six or seven witches. The boy was a member of a family long suspected of witchery and his mother was hanged for it in the autumn of 1645. Although the boy admitted sending an imp to kill chickens, he was released because both the jury and Stearne had hopes of his amendment. They were wrong. Again he got involved with the Devil who appeared to him in the form of a mare which carried him wherever he wanted to go.

Elizabeth Deekes, 'a silly ignorant young woman' from Rattlesden, said she was drawn into it by her mother and confessed to using her two crop-eared mouse imps 'to the much prejudice of her neighbours and townsmen'.

In many cases the scenario was just as the Tudor sceptic Reginald Scot had described in the previous century when he wrote, 'She was at my house of late, she would have had a pot of milk, she departed in a chafe because she had it not, she cursed, she mumbled and whispered, and finally she said she would be even with me: and soon after my child, my cow, my sow, or my pullet died, or was strangely taken. Nay, if it please your worship, I have further proof: I was with a wise woman and she told me I had an ill neighbour and that she would come to my house yet it were long, and so did she, and that she had a mark above her waist, and so had she: and God forgive me, my stomach has gone against her a great while. Her mother before her was counted a witch, she has been beaten and scratched by the face till blood was drawn because she has been suspected and afterwards some of those persons were said to amend.' One such case was that of old Anne Randell of Lavenham who confessed to having imps called Hangman and Jacob in the form of blue kittens. William Baldwin refused to give her some wood until she paid for a previous load so she sent Hangman to kill his horses. The imp killed the horses and everyone thought they had died in a thunderstorm. She went begging to another man's house and he 'gave her such words as she liked not' so she sent Hangman to kill one his hogs.

The result of all the searching, walking, swimming and watching by Hopkins and his associates was that about 120 people were taken into custody in Suffolk but the trials seem to have been abruptly ended 'by reason of the near approaching of the Cavaliers'. A Royalist force had moved south from Lincolnshire and had scattered a small force of Roundheads before briefly occupying Huntingdon. The panic quickly subsided and in fact the war was coming to an end. In June Prince Rupert had taken Leicester only to be defeated in a decisive battle at Naseby later in the month. Rupert was held in particular terror by many on Parliament's side and some of the Halesworth witches were said to have sent imps to help him.

The mass trial of witches at Bury St Edmunds attracted plenty of attention and a pamphlet was published about it. Its title page reads, 'A true Relation of the Arraignment of eighteen Witches that were tried, convicted, and condemned, at a Sessions holden at St Edmundsbury in Suffolk, and there by the Judge and Justices of the said Sessions condemned to die, and so were executed the 27 day of August 1645. As also a list of the names of those that were executed, and their several confessions before their executions. With a true relation of the manner how they find them out. The names of those that were executed, Mr Lowes parson of Branson, Thomas Everred a cooper with Mary his wife, Mary Bacon, Anne Alderman, Rebecca Morris, Mary Fuller, Mary Clowes, Margery Sparham, Katherine Tooley, Sarah Spinlow, Jane Limstead, Anne Wright, Mary Smith, Jane Rivers, Susan Manners, Mary Skipper, Anne Leech.'

By autumn criticism to the witch-hunts was being voiced with greater confidence. A London publication called *The Moderate Intelligencer* appeared with the comment, 'Religious men say Devils are wiser than men but why then is it that Devils should choose to be conversant with silly women. If the devil be so wise and wise to do evil why should he not choose to deal with wise men and great men. Yet as appears by the news we receive this day from Suffolk he meddles with none but poor old women. Life is precious and there is need of great inquisition before it is taken away.'

Parson Lowes had been but one of many who had had their thumbs tied to their toes and then tossed into Framlingham mere to see if they would sink or float. Ten or more women from the town were accused of witchcraft and among them were Mary Edwards, Elizabeth Warne and Margery Chinery who were said to have bewitched children after arguments with the townspeople or disputes over milk and rent. After being watched for three days and two nights Ellen Driver ended her torment by saying she had been married to the Devil for sixty years, that he had cloven feet and that they had lived together and had children but they were changelings. Such sexual fantasies, whether volunteered or suggested by the watchers, are a recurring feature of English and Scottish witch trial evidence. The Devil, said some women, appeared to them as handsome, well-dressed young men or boys, usually with a hollow voice. In many instances the women were obviously recounting previous sexual encounters. Poor and illiterate women sometimes had to turn to occasional prostitution and those experiences may have been the basis of some of their confessions. Witch suspects were often women of ill repute who were called drab, dell, mort, doxie, wanton, strumpet or harlot by their accusers.

Many of the confessions served to illustrate the abject poverty of most of the men and women who were caught up in the witch-hunt. That of Joan Ruce of Polstead was typical. She was in a field one day when she saw six chickens under a bush. She caught three and took them home where they turned into imps like mice called Touch, Pluck and Take. Then in a 'great hollow voice' [the Devil and all his imps seem to have spoken with a deep hollow voice] she was told that if she denied God and Christ 'she should never want meat, drink or clothes or money'. She then sealed the pact with six drops of blood from one finger.

Joan Beales of Wickham was watched for three days and admitted keeping imps although she would not say exactly how many, but the number was 'not above three'. One watcher was a cleric who told her to defy the Devil when he thought he detected an evil spirit in the room. He described her as an Anabaptist and 'runner after the new sects.' Beales' daughter Mary Brame said her mother gave her some imps so that 'she should never want and be revenged on her enemies.' She added that on the second night when she and her watchers fell asleep her imps came and woke her and she suckled them.

Mary Bush of Bacton said the Devil appeared at her bedside in the shape of a young black man soon after her husband's death some fifteen years previously. He would kiss her and then they had sex two or three times a week but she found him a disappointing lover saying 'he was colder than man, and heavier, and could not perform nature as man'. She had two imps like mice and she sent one to torment a maid servant who was against her being given charity by her master.

But the spell did not last long because the servant came looking for Bush and when she found her she scratched her till she drew blood and that ended the bewitchment.

Elizabeth Southern had been walking across Westleton Heath when the Devil appeared as a boy 'hairy though young' and he had promised her 2s 6d. The Devil in the guise of a man lay in the bushes with Margaret Bennet of Bacton and then scratched her and wrote 'she knew not what.' Satan came to Margaret Wyard of Framlingham as 'a handsome young gentleman with yellow hair and black clothes' and cloven feet and he 'had the carnal use of her'. This description of the Devil is different to the more usual 'ugly devil having horns on his head, fire in his mouth, and a tail in his breech, eyes like a basin, fangs like a dog, claws like a bear, a skin like a nigger and a voice roaring like a lion.' Wyard said the Devil had warned her a month in advance that a man would come searching for witches but she was not to fear. Again the witch-hunters gleefully reported that all the Devil's promises proved false, whether they were for protection, money or food. And having it told that the Devil was warning his 'darlings' of the witchfinder's approach would have done Hopkins' reputation no harm.

Ellen Greenleaf of Bacton 'confessed that when she prayed she prayed to the Devil and not to God'. She said she plagued her neighbours with lice and lamed a farmer's mare because he had sent for Hopkins. After being 'watched' Faith Mills of Fressingfield confessed to causing a farmer's cow to jump over a stile, a horse to throw its rider and a cart to stand immovable. Ellen Crisp of Sweffling was accused because she and her parents were 'commonly reputed' to be witches. A widow from near Hadleigh was said to have plagued a man with lice after he refused her some wood chippings for her fire from a tree he was felling. Alexander Sussums of Long Melford said it should be no surprise to anyone if he were a witch because it ran in the family and three of his relatives – his mother, aunt and grandmother – had been executed for the crime. After three nights of being watched Shotley widow Margaret Mixter had convulsions and hallucinations. She thought she was possessed by the

Devil and had to be held down. A witness said something strange came from under her skirts and vanished. The watchers said it must have been one of her imps but she said it was one of her neighbour's chickens.

In September 1645 Mary Lakeland, the widow of Ipswich barber John Lakeland, was convicted and burned to death. She was executed by burning instead of hanging because her offences included the murder of her husband and that was petty treason. She said she had been a witch for twenty years and the Devil had sealed their pact with her blood after scratching her with his claw. A pamphlet about the case said 'he furnished her with three imps, two little dogs and a mole, which she employed in her service. Her husband she bewitched whereby he lay in great misery for a time and at last died. Then she sent one of her dogs to Mr Lawrence of Ipswich, to torment him and take away his life; she sent one of them also to his child to torment it and take away the life of it, which was done upon them both; and all this was because he asked her for twelve shillings that she owed him, and for no other cause. She further confessed that she sent her mole to a maid of one Mrs Jennings in Ipswich to torment her and take away her life, which was done accordingly, and this for no other cause but for that the said maid would not lend her a needle that she desired to borrow of her, and was earnest with her for a shilling which she owed the said maid.'

It was also said that Mother Lakeland had taken revenge on a man who had stopped his courtship of her granddaughter. 'Because he would not have her, she sent and burnt a new ship that had never been to sea, that he was to go master of; and sent also to torment him and take away his life; but he is yet living but in very great misery, and it is vainly conceived by the doctors and chirugeons that have him in hand that he consumes and rots, and that half of his body is rotten upon him as he is living. Several other things she did for all which she was by law condemned to die, and in particular to be burnt to death, because she was the death of her husband which death she suffered accordingly.' Her death resulted in 'one thing that is very remarkable, and to be taken notice of: that upon the very day that she was burned, a bunch of flesh, something after the form of a dog, that grew upon the thigh of the said Mr Beale, ever since the time that she first sent her imp to him being very hard but could never be made to break by all the means that could be used, break of itself without any means using. And another sore that at the same time she sent her imp to him rose upon the side of his belly in the form of a fistula, which ran and could not be broken for all the means that could be used, presently also began to heal, and that there is great hope that he will suddenly recover again, for his sores heal apace and he doth recover his strength. He was in this misery for the space of a year and a half, and was forced to go with his head and his knees together, his misery was so great.'

Exactly how many Suffolk witches were executed as a result of the activities of Hopkins and Stearne is not known. Eighteen were hanged in one day at Bury St Edmunds and Stearne said the number condemned was sixty-eight. Writing some years after the events the poet Samuel Butler and Squire Revett of Brandeston said that about sixty were actually executed.

Within a matter of months Hopkins' reputation as a witchfinder was such that towns and villages were virtually begging him to come and rid them of their witches. In May 1646 the civic leaders of King's Lynn decided 'to send for Mr Hopkins the witch discoverer and his charges and recompense to be borne by the town.' Hopkins obliged with a visit in September and two women were hanged for witches. One newsletter claimed that by late summer of 1645 twenty witches had been hanged in Norfolk. In August the leading men of Great Yarmouth invited the witchfinder to come and search for witches in their town, the corporation resolving that 'the gentleman Mr Hopkins being employed in the county for discovering and finding out witches, be sent for to search for such wicked persons, if any be, and have his fee and allowances for his pains, as he has in other places.' The civic fathers agreed to pay the women who searched suspects for imp teats a shilling a day. Hopkins obliged by finding sixteen suspects and five or six were hanged. Hopkins told Stearne that one of the miscreants had made a clay picture of her intended child victim, stuck a nail in the head and buried it. Stearne wrote, 'I was told by Master Hopkin who was there and took her confession and went to look for the picture and that the child (as I have heard) did soon after mend and grew lusty again. A hellish invention.' The unluckiest Norfolk 'witch' was a baker by the name of Meggs who lived near Norwich. He volunteered to be searched for marks, was found to have them and was hanged. Another man who volunteered to be searched for marks was Alexander Sussums from Long Melford in Suffolk. Stearne duly found the incriminating marks and Sussums confessed to being a witch, a fate he said he could not avoid because he had been brought up in a family of witches. He pleaded, 'He could not help it, for that all his generation was naught [worthless]; and so told me his mother and aunt were hanged, his grandmother burnt for witchcraft, and others of them questioned and hanged'. Sussums was tried but despite confessing to having kept imps for more than sixteen years he was freed, no doubt much to Stearne's dismay.

In 1646 Hopkins and Stearne turned their attentions to Cambridgeshire, Bedfordshire and Huntingdonshire and more unfortunate people were hanged. But the number involved was much smaller and the witchfinders were finding that their critics were becoming more outspoken. No longer could they use the swimming test and their activities were viewed with increasing hostility. The mood of the country was changing as the fighting between Cavaliers and Roundheads came to an end with the surrender of the last Royalist force at Stow on the Wold in March 1646.

In his *Historical Essay Concerning Witchcraft* of 1718, Bishop Hutchinson wrote of the opposition Hopkins had encountered in 1646. 'Matthew Hopkins of Manningtree in Essex, and one John Stern, and a woman [Mary Philips] along with them, went round from town to town through many parts of Essex, Suffolk, Norfolk and Huntingdonshire to discover witches. Several clergymen preached and spake against them, as far as those times would suffer, and particularly Mr Gaul of Staughton in Huntingdonshire, opposed very heartily that trade that those people drove.'

John Gaule was a minister of Puritan leanings and he published what he preached. His objections were printed in 1646 in a booklet entitled *Select Cases of Conscience Concerning Witches*. Hopkins knew of Gaule's contempt for his 'trade' and his methods when he wrote a letter containing anti-Royalist rhetoric to a magistrate in which he declared his intention to make a sudden visit 'to search for evil disposed persons called witches' in Great Staughton. Although he knew parson Gaule was 'far against us through ignorance' he said it was his hope to be able to go about his work 'without control'.

Hopkins wrote, 'My service to your Worship presented, I have this day received a letter to come to a town called Great Staughton to search for evil disposed persons called witches (though I hear your minister is far against us through ignorance). I intend to come (God willing) the sooner to hear his singular judgement on the behalf of such parties. I have known a minister in Suffolk preach as much against their discovery in a pulpit, and forced to recant it by the Committee in the same place...

I intend to give your town a visit suddenly. I am to come to Kimbolton this week, and it shall be ten to one but I will come to your town first; but I would certainly know afore whether your town affords many sticklers for such cattle, or is willing to give and afford us good welcome and entertainment, as others where I have been, else I shall wave your shire (not as yet beginning in any part of it myself) and betake me to such places where I do, and may persist without control, but with thanks and recompense. So I humbly take my leave and rest. Your servant to be commanded, Matthew Hopkins.'

Seven or eight witches were discovered in the cluster of villages of Bythorn, Great and Little Catworth, Molesworth and Keyston, all of them only a few miles from Great Staughton. They were tried and executed at Huntingdon. One was widow Elizabeth Weed of Great Catworth whose old pet dogs Lily and Priscill were pronounced to be imps, one specialising in injuring people and the other cattle. She confessed 'the Devil offered her that he would do what mischief she should require him, and said she must covenant with him that he must have her soul at the end of one and twenty years which she granted.' Molesworth labourer John Winnick said he had been to meetings of witches where as many as 'above fourscore' were assembled. He said he made a pact with the Devil when a spirit like a black shaggy bear appeared and helped him to find his lost purse. Joan Wallis, Elizabeth Chandler and John Clarke all lived in Keyston and they were accused and convicted of witchcraft. Stearne described Wallis as 'a very ignorant sottish woman' and claimed that she confessed that the Devil came to her in the likeness of a man in black clothes with cloven feet. He gave her two imps called Grizzell and Greedigut and had the use of her body although he was uglier than any man.

John Clarke was a young labourer who came from a family of reputed witches and he thought he could beat the witchfinders at their own game by cutting off his marks. But Stearne was not to be fooled and Clarke admitted that he had cut off the marks on his body three days before he was searched. Alice Marsh of Bramford was searched two or three times without any witch marks being found on her body. But one of her neighbours continued to accuse her of being a witch so the constables arrested her again when she was not expecting it. This time the marks were found and she confessed that she had been caught only because she was not wearing her special shift which hid her marks.

The fact that some men and women would cut off any marks on their bodies illustrates the terror that was raised in some men and women. Stearne said that a woman from Over in Cambridgeshire 'plucked her marks off the night before' but it did not stop Stearne getting a confession that her imps had harmed several of her neighbours including the local magistrate.

Frances Moore of Little Catworth confessed that her two imps had been given to her by two local women. One imp was a black puppy which she named Pretty and one a white cat called Tissy. Ellen Shepherd of Molesworth said she had received her three rat imps from the Devil who promised her 'all happiness' when she was cursing and swearing in a field. Anne Desborough of Bythorn said her imps were mice called Tib and Joan and she had made her pact with

94

the Devil some thirty years before when she was living at Titchmarsh. Two or three others from nearby places in Northamptonshire were arrested. One was 'a young man of Denford' who was hanged for sending an imp to stampede a man's cattle, and another 'a very aged man of Thrapston' called Cherrie who died in jail on the day he was due to be tried. One of his neighbours had 'died in a miserable condition' after a quarrel in which Cherrie had said that he hoped the man's tongue would 'rot out of his head.'

The confessions became more and more incredible. Two witnesses watching a woman from Keyston believed that she sat in her chair and did not move, but two other witnesses saw her go outside into the yard and then back indoors. The suspect explained that the Devil took on her likeness and sat in the chair while she did indeed go outside to suckle her imps. Stearne related the remarkable story of a woman who lived in St Neots who apparently turned into a dog. She had been body searched two or three times but no witch marks were found and then she was swum and although she floated 'she was not further meddled with'. Some time later one of the townsmen who had long suspected that she was a witch saw a dog come into his yard which his own guard dog refused to approach. His son hit the strange dog which was then bitten and shaken by another dog before running off. When the suspected witch was not seen about town she was searched again and was found to have lots of bites and bruises on her neck and body.

John Wynnick admitted that one day he lost his purse and seven shillings in a barn in Thrapston and he got in an angry rage about it. He said he would go to a cunning man for help if only he knew one and he continued cursing and swearing so much that the Devil appeared in the form of a bear about the size of a rabbit. The next day he returned to the barn and found his purse, and the small bear turned into a rat and sealed their pact by drawing some blood from the side of his head.

Several men and women from the Cambridgeshire fenlands were charged with witchcraft crimes and perhaps as many as eight were executed shortly before Michaelmas 1647. Among the places involved were Chatteris, Ely, Haddenham, Sutton and Stretham. The case of a woman called Lendall from Cambridge produced an outrageous and amusing piece of evidence. It was said that an old male witch was riding to a meeting of witches on the back of a black hog but he flew too close to Great Shelford church tower and tore his breeches on the weather vane. The idea of witches travelling on the backs of hogs was not new and Hopkins and his cronies may have picked it up from gossip about earlier incidents. A pamphlet about the execution of five witches at Northampton in July 1612 had shown the three from Guilsborough, all described as 'loose women', perched on the back of a pig. The following year three were hanged at Bedford and one of them, Mary Sutton, who was swum twice in the millpond and floated 'like a plank', was said to have gone like a black sow to scare a farmer's animals.

By the end of 1646 Hopkins' career as a witchfinder was virtually over. Popular enthusiasm for witch-hunting was dying away and witch-hunter-in-chief Matthew Hopkins was dying too. The normal structures for the administration of justice had returned after the breakdown of the law during the Civil War and the regular calendar of county assizes controlled by professional judges was quickly reinstated. Judges at the Norfolk Assizes had been left with the task of clearing up after Hopkins' witch-finding forays into the county and they began to raise questions about his competence and authority. The sceptical and dissenting voices within the legal establishment, a growing sense of public rejection plus a mounting tide of criticism among religious leaders stung Hopkins and his reply was to hastily pen an angry reply.

The result was the publication in London in May 1647 of a pamphlet entitled *The Discovery of Witches*. [The full text is printed at the end of this book] It seethes with Hopkins' arrogance and anger as he attempts to dismiss the criticism levelled against him and shift the blame for any cruelty onto the shoulders of others.

The format of his treatise is, like King James's book *Daemonologie*, a series of questions and answers and they give an insight into what was being said about him when he was at the height of his power. The gossip was that surely he must have come face to face with the Devil and cheated him of his book in which were written the names of every witch in England. Indeed it was said that he could tell who was a witch just by looking at people. His answer in dismissive. If he had outwitted the Devil then that must be to his credit, and as for 'judgement in physiognomy', he claimed that he was no better at it than any other man. His skill as a witchfinder came not 'from his profound learning or from much reading of learned authors concerning that subject' but from experience 'which though it be meanly esteemed of' was the 'surest and safest way to judge by'. The experience he had gained, he said, could be acquired by anyone.

He relates how and why the Manningtree witch-hunt began and states that Elizabeth Clarke was kept awake for several nights 'upon command from the Justice'. He attempts to explain how witches' marks and Devil's marks can be distinguished from natural ones. He defends the use of the 'swimming' test but adds that it was never used as evidence of guilt at a witch's trial and that he stopped using it as soon as 'able divines whom I reverence' banned it. He claims that much of the 'unreasonable watching' and the walking of suspects till their feet blistered had been the result of 'rustical people' misusing, spoiling and abusing suspects contrary to the true meaning of his instructions. He claims that he 'is of a better conscience' than to allow the torture to 'wring out a word or two of confession from any of these stupefied, ignorant, unintelligible, poor silly creatures. Confessions gained by torture, violence or flattery had no validity and that he had dismissed confessions of anything that was improbable or impossible like flying through the air on a broom.

He concludes by responding to the claim that he had only done it for the money. 'All that the witch-finder does is to fleece the country of their money and therefore rides and goes to town to have employment, and promises them fair promises, and it may be does nothing for it, and possesses [encourages] many men that they have so many wizards and so many witches in their town, and so heartens them on they entertain him.' His answer was that he only went to places that had sent for him and were glad to see him. As for enriching himself he answers, 'Consider the vast sum he takes of every town. He demands but 20 shillings a town and does sometimes ride twenty miles for that and has no more for all his charges [expenses] there and back again, and perhaps stay a week there and find three or four witches, or if it be but one, cheap enough, and this is the great sum he takes to maintain his company with three horses.'

The Discovery of Witches was a blustering attempt by an arrogant bully who relished the taste of power. The fact that he felt compelled to write it indicates the extent to which his popular support had ebbed away as the self-appointed saviour had become a man despised by many.

John Stearne continued the witch-hunt for a few months into 1647 in the face of the mounting opposition. He took the hunt into the isolated and suspicious communities of the Fens but he found that the enthusiasm for witch-hunting was waning there too and the number of victims was only about a dozen.

Matthew Hopkins died at his home and the parish register of St Mary's, Mistley-cum-Manningtree recorded his burial on August 12, 1647 – 'Matthew son of Mr James Hopkings [sic], minister of Wenham, buried at Mistley.' It has been claimed that such was his infamy that he was buried unmourned at night. Mistley church of Hopkins' time decayed and was replaced in 1735 by a building which Robert Adam was asked to improve. Only Adam's towers remain of that church and its Victorian replacement stands near Mistley pond.

But did Hopkins really die in his bed? Bishop Hutchinson heard a very different story. He wrote, 'What I have often heard is that Hopkins went on searching and swimming poor creatures until some gentleman, out of indignation at the barbarity, took him and tied his own thumbs and toes, as he used to tie others, and when he was put into water, he himself swam as they did. That cleared the country of him; and it was a great deal of pity that they did not think of the experiment sooner.'

For what it is worth legend offers various other versions of his end. Among them are that he was seized by a vengeful mob, swum, tried and hanged but there is no record of Hopkins being tried and executed by either a vigilante crowd or by the authorities, or that he was swum and drowned in the process. Places mentioned in connection with this mythical swimming include Mistley pond and the 'witch's pool' of the river Waveney near Harleston. It has even been suggested that he took ship to America to escape reprisal and was involved in the infamous Salem witch trials of 1692.

The road from Manningtree to Mistley is known as the Walls and it passes Mistley Pond which drains into the River Stour. Local legend points to this as being the site of Hopkins' floating and death. The location is known as 'Hoppin Bridge' which some people suggest is a corruption of 'Hopkins Bridge'. Could this be an example of the final act in his life being preserved by local folk memory? And there have been numerous reported sightings of the ghost of the Witchfinder General appearing at this spot.

In September 1647 the last witches 'discovered' by Hopkins and Stearne went to the gallows and Stearne quietly retired to the village of Lawshall near Bury St Edmunds. There he wrote his account of what had happened and it was published in London in 1648.

He called his book *A Confirmation and Discovery of Witchcraft* and declared that it contained 'these several particulars; that there are Witches called bad witches and witches untruly called good or white witches, and what manner of people they be, and how they may be known, with many particulars thereunto tending. Together with the Confessions of many of those executed since May 1645 in the several counties hereafter mentioned'.

Stearne's book – and it is a book some ten times longer than Hopkins' hurriedly written and blame-shifting treatise – is a considered and generally calmly presented piece peppered with biblical references and quotations. Stearne's religious stance is immediately obvious. He sees sin and the Devil's hand everywhere. 'Man is naturally wholly polluted with sin and corruption whereby he is become of very near kin unto the Devil,' he writes. 'For Satan has his wiles, his devices, his depths and policies, his snares to catch people at unawares......not only with the rude and sottish but with the greatest spirits and sharpest wits. For man being given over to his unruly passion, is violent, inconsiderate and vehemently greedy to have his desired ends by what means soever he can attain them, which makes him seek means of the Devil to become enjoyer of his inordinate desires, regarding more the having of his present will than respecting his future state after death.'

Like Hopkins, one of Stearne's motives for going into print was to answer their critics. 'Now the occasion being thus offered, and Master Hopkins dead, I desire to give some satisfaction to the world, that it may appear what has been done has been for the good of the commonwealth,' he wrote and added, 'I know many in the world will be ready enough to censure of me.' And in Stearne's view what they had done was God's work. 'And surely let no man doubt but that the finding out of such miscreants is an acceptable service before God,' he declared.

He defends his favourite way of witch finding by stating that body searches for witch marks 'is both the most ready and certain way and if they which undertake it be careful, there can be no mistake.'

On the subject of forcing confessions by watching and keeping, he asserts that such a thing would be against his Christian principles. 'I desire to answer one objection before I proceed further. That is, some say, and many will and do say: but you watched them and kept them from meat, drink or rest and so made them say what you would.' He claims that he never knew of a suspect being deprived of meat, drink or rest. Indeed he states that 'they had better provision, either meat or drink, than at their own houses.'

As for swimming, he declares that it was only resorted to in the early days of the witch-hunt when the weather was at its warmest so ' none took any harm by it, neither did I ever do it but upon their own request'. His answer to the charge that he was motivated by money was, 'I call God to witness that considering the charge of going to several places, and assizes and gaol deliveries, and the time I expended thereabouts, I never got so much as I did by my calling and practice towards the maintenance of my family. And as for taking any money or other thing by way of bribe or gift, I never did to the value of one penny, but what I openly took in the view of the townsmen where I came. In many places I never received a penny.'

The opprobrium that had become attached to his and Hopkins' names rankled deeply with Stearne. He ends his books with the words, 'And in truth, concerning him who is dead, who likewise was an agent in the business [Hopkins], for my part I never knew that he either unjustly favoured any, or received bribes, or used such extremity as was reported of him. At first before he or I ever went, many towns used extremity of themselves, which after was laid on us. And I do not deny but at first he might watch some, but to my knowledge he soon left it, or at least in such a way as not to make them incapable. But if he ever did evidence was not taken till after they rested . And for my part, I never watched any at first so as any way at all to disturb them in their brains. But now lately and ever since the Michaelmas after the first beginning [autumn 1645], I never used any but as aforesaid, with consent of the Justice and not otherwise, nor ever did. But to my knowledge we have been both much injured in words, and he since his death. But I am certain (notwithstanding whatsoever has been said of him) he died peaceably at Manningtree, after a long sickness of a consumption, as many of his generation had done before him, without any trouble of conscience for what he had done, as was falsely reported of him. And though many of these things may seem very strange and hardly to be believed, yet this is the very truth; and that he was the son of a godly minister and therefore without doubt within the Covenant. Therefore let no man take upon him either to speak or write more than he knows to be truth, for this I am able to manifest and prove to be truth. And so I leave myself to the censure of the world, yet desire it might be left to the Almighty who knows the secrets of all hearts: For blessed are they that do his commandments, Revel 22.14.'

Hopkins and Stearne were unrepentant about their witch-hunting to the end. Stearne maintained his belief by stating, 'Everyone must conclude with me that (as yet) of witchcrafts there is no end' and consumption [tuberculosis] hurried Hopkins to an early grave. So in one sense Hopkins may indeed have been a victim of his own witch-hunt. Stearne eventually returned to Manningtree and drifted into obscurity, his name remembered only by his association with Hopkins.

Tucked away in Hopkins' pamphlet is a short and indignant paragraph which perhaps sheds a little more light on the tensions that existed in Manningtree in the weeks leading up to start of the witch-hunt. 'Observe this generation of witches,' Hopkins wrote. 'If they be at any time abused by being called whore, thief etc by any where they live, they are the readiest to cry and wring their hands, and shed tears in abundance, and run with full and right sorrowful acclamations to some Justice of Peace, and with many tears make their complaints…'

In Manningtree and in a thousand other places differences in religious enthusiasm and belief ran deep. So too did the divisions in attitudes to sex and work as well as those caused by extremes of poverty, and all were exacerbated by the upheavals and pressures generated by civil war. The witch-hunt that flared up in Manningtree in 1645 could have started in any one of a score or more other towns and villages across East Anglia. The difference was that in Manningtree there was a man ready to step forward and take charge when he saw the first sparks begin to fly. And his name was Matthew Hopkins.

Places and numbers caught up in the Suffolk witch-hunt included – thirteen women from Framlingham; ten women and a man from Glemham; eight women from Aldeburgh; four women, two men and a boy from Rattlesden; five women and two men from Halesworth; five women and a man from Ipswich; four women and two men from both Bramford and Stowmarket; five women from Wickham [Market], four women from each of Bacton, Chattisham, Copdock, Hintlesham; three women from Rushmere; two women from each of Belstead, Creeting, Dunwich, Hitcham, Lavenham, Playford and Wetherden. Other places involved included Acton, Blaxhall, Brandeston, Bungay, Coddenham, Combs, Flowton, Fressingfield, Great Waldingfield, Haverhill, Linstead, Melford, Mendham, Metfield, Mettingham, Offton, Polstead, Shelley, Shotley, Stradbroke, Sudbury, Sweffling, Tattingstone, Wattisham, Westleton, Westhorpe and Wingfield.

Brandeston Church in Suffolk where John Lowes was vicar for almost 50 years. Unfortunately for Mr Lowes, many of his parishioners wanted to be rid of him and the Hopkins witch-hunt gave them the chance to do so. He was swum at Framlingham and later hanged at Bury St Edmunds after having read his own burial service.

Hudibras and Sidrophel

*T*wo men who lived through the years of the Hopkins witch-hunt and had profoundly different views on just about everything were Samuel Butler, the poet and satirist, and Laurence Claxton [or Clarkson], the 'prodigal' who, in his own words, 'made many a sad and weary journey through many religious countries'. Their lives and works illustrate the religious ferment that was the background to the Hopkins witch-hunt.

Born in 1612, Butler was a man whose talents were never truly recognised or rewarded during his lifetime and he died in poverty in 1680. His greatest monument is *Hudibras*, a long satirical poem of 11,316 lines aimed at religious hypocrisy, superstition, magic, and the gullibility that allowed quacks, astrologers and fortune tellers to prosper. He ridiculed the astrologer and publisher of predictions William Lilly in the guise of the character Sidrophel in the poem. Another target was Nicholas Fiske, once of Framlingham, who found fame and fortune in London telling fortunes, casting nativities, and dabbling in astrology and medicine. In the 16th and early 17th century superstition prospered under many guises.

Butler believed that mankind created its own fears and he makes mention of many of the supposed skills of the fortune tellers and astrologers –

> They'll search a Planet's House to know
> Who broke and robb'd a House below:
> Examine Venus, and the Moon,
> Who stole a Thimble or a Spoon:
> And tho' they nothing will confess,
> Yet by their very Looks can guess,
> And tell what guilty Aspect bodes,
> Who stole, and who receiv'd the Goods.
> They'll question Mars, and, by his Look,

Detect who 'twas that nimm'd a Cloke:
Make Mercury confess, and 'peach
Those Thieves which he himself did teach.
They'll find, i' the Physiognomies
O' th' Planets, all Men's Destinies;
Like him that took the Doctor's Bill,
And swallow'd it instead o' th' Pill:
Cast the Nativity o' th' Question,
And from Positions to be guess'd on,
As sure as if they knew the Moment
Of Native's Birth, tell what will come on't.
They'll feel the Pulses of the Stars,
To find out Agues, Coughs, Catarrhs;
And tell what Crisis does divine
The Rot in Sheep, or Mange in Swine;
In Men, what gives or cures the Itch,
What makes them Cuckolds, poor or rich:
What gains or loses, hangs or saves;
What makes Men great, what Fools or Knaves,
But not what wise; for only of those
The Stars (they say) cannot dispose.

Cunning men were another of his targets and he ridiculed their methods and their remedies –

Detect lost Maiden-Heads [virginity] by Sneezing,
Or breaking Wind of Dames, or Pissing;
Cure Warts and Corns, with Application
Of Med'cines to th' Imagination;
Fright Agues into Dogs, and scare
With Rhimes the Tooth-Ach and Catarrh:
Chace evil Spirits away by Dint
Of Cickle, Horse-Shoe, Hollow-Flint.

Butler believed that the human mind could invent more terrors than any witch –

Who wou'd believe what strange Bugbears
Mankind creates itself, of Fears
That spring, like Fern, that insect Weed,
Equivocally, without Seed?
And have no possible Foundation,
But meerly in th' Imagination?
And yet can do more dreadful Feats
Than Hags, with all their Imps and Teats;
Make more bewitch and haunt themselves,
Than all their Nurseries of Elves.
For Fear does Things so like a Witch,
Tis hard t' unriddle which is which.

But to come to his reference to Hopkins. Butler satirised the hypocrisy of Puritan fanatics [the Saints he called them] by making them claim that they could and would deal with the Devil if it suited their purpose, a crime for which they eagerly hanged others.

Some lines from Butler's works were placed with the parish records of Brandeston, the village that for many years had been the home of Hopkins' most prominent victim, the old parson John Lowes. Butler's poem has well over one hundred references to the Devil, witches and witchcraft, cunning men, imps and conjurors and he lampoons the infamous witchfinder, his methods and his supposed fate.

Quoth Hudibras, This Sidrophel
I've heard of, and should like it well,
If thou canst prove the Saints have Freedom
To go to Sorc'rers when they need 'em.
Says Ralpho, There's no Doubt of that;
Those Principles I quoted late,

Prove that the Godly may alledge
For any Thing their Priviledge;
And to the Dev'l himself may go,
If they have Motives thereunto.
For, as there is a War between
The Dev'l and them, it is no Sin,
If they, by subtle Stratagem,
Make use of him, as he does them.
Has not this present Parliament
A Ledger to the Devil sent,
Fully impower'd to treat about
Finding revolted Witches out?
And has not he, within a Year,
Hang'd threescore of 'em in one Shire?
Some only for not being drown'd,
And some for sitting above Ground,
Whole Days and Nights, upon their Breeches,
And feeling Pain, were hang'd for Witches:
And some for putting knavish Tricks
Upon Green Geese, and Turky Chicks,
Or Pigs, that suddenly deceast
Of Griefs unnat'ral, as he guest;
Who after prov'd himself a Witch,
And made a Rod for his own Breech.

Only a decade after Hopkins and Stearne had faded from the scene one of the most notable religious eccentrics of the Commonwealth and Cromwellian period was earning his living as a cunning man and trying to meet the Devil in the heart of Suffolk where once the witch-hunters had detected many of their victims.

Laurence Clarkson was born in 1615 in Preston and 'educated in the form and worship of the Church of England'. He was a genuine radical and he turned to many brands of religion – Presbyterian, Independent, Baptist, Seeker, Ranter, Muggletonian. His unorthodox and often licentious lifestyle led him into many confrontations with the authorities and at one point he was imprisoned in Bury St Edmunds only a few months before the Hopkins witch-hunt began. It was claimed that he 'dipped' [baptised] men and women naked in the night. Clarkson died in 1667 while in prison for debt.

He travelled widely through East Anglia as a soldier, priest and preacher, and for a time he practised 'the art of astrology and physic, which in a short time I gained, and therewith travelled up and down Cambridgeshire and Essex, as Linton and Saffron Walden and other country towns, improving my skill to the utmost that I had clients many.'

Clarkson turned his hand to magic, read some old books about it and then openly practised his new skills while he lived in the Glemsford and Lavenham area. He wrote, 'I improved my genius to fetch goods back that were stolen, yea to raise spirits and fetch treasure out of the earth with many such diabolical actions as a woman of Sudbury in Suffolk assisted me, pretending she could do by her witchcraft whatever she pleased. Monies I gained and was up and down looked upon as a dangerous man so that the ignorant and religious people were afraid to come near me.' He claimed that he 'cured many desperate diseases' and on one frosty night returned the bewitched daughter of a doctor to perfect health. That, said Clarkson, 'puffed up my spirit and made many fools believe in me....I several times attempted to raise the devil that so I might see what he was, but all in vain, so that I judged all was a lie and that there was no devil at all, nor indeed no God but only nature.' But Clarkson's days as a Suffolk cunning man were numbered and he returned to preaching, taking up positions at Terrington St John and Snettisham before returning to London.

The large and imposing memorial statue to Lord Chief Justice Sir John Holt which stands in the village church at Redgrave in Suffolk. Sir John presided over several witch trial in the closing years of the 17th Century, all of which ended in acquittal. Sir John was very influential in bringing witch prosecutions in England to an end. He died in 1710.

Defiance to the March of Intellect

*I*n the spring of 1647 when Matthew Hopkins published his tract on the 'horrible and damnable sin of witchcraft', a labourer from his hometown of Manningtree appeared in court at Chelmsford charged with bewitching a boy to death. He was acquitted, and so too was a woman on a similar charge. At the next Essex Assizes in August a man and a woman from Navestock were cleared of bewitchment and the next day, August 12, Matthew Hopkins, the witchfinder general, was dead and buried. Tradition claims that his name had become so notorious and his death was so unlamented that he was buried at night. Be that as it may, from that moment the witchcraft superstition went into an irreversible retreat in England.

There were more executions but the trend was for indictments of witchcraft to be declared 'no true bills'. The Hopkins episode had been a cruel aberration in which he and his associates had been responsible for around two hundred deaths in two years. Stearne claimed 'about two hundred in number were justly and deservedly executed upon their legal trials.' Within a few years the civil wars were at an end, the monarchy was restored, 'enthusiastic' brands of religion fell out of fashion, and witch-mania returned to the slowly decaying state it had been in before the struggle between King and Parliament.

It had been the tensions of conflict – social, military, religious and political – which had allowed Hopkins to emerge from obscurity and ride high on an upsurge of the forces of ignorance and intolerance. Somewhat similar circumstances occurred again in England later in the 17th century, but by then belief in witchcraft among the policy-makers of the establishment had decayed beyond resurrection in such a virulent form. Never again would there be mass trials of twenty or thirty supposed witches at a time.

But, unfortunately, belief in witchery and the methods Hopkins had used to detect it did not perish with him.

What happened was that judges and juries became more impartial and less credulous. There were exceptions, but generally speaking English courts became reluctant to hang people for a crime which was impossible to prove by rational means and was founded on an increasingly disputed theology. By the closing years of the 17th century, witchcraft, once an offence against God, had become an offence to the march of intellect. Those who attempted to maintain the belief found the tide flowing ever more strongly against them and by the end of that century the cause was lost, at least in the courts. This was demonstrated in 1693 when Samuel Petto, a clergyman from Sudbury in Suffolk, published a tract bewailing the failure of a case involving 'the wonderful and extraordinary fits which Mr Thomas Spatchett was under by witchcraft'. Although the defendant confessed to keeping imps, the reverend gentleman wrote 'that notwithstanding what could be witnessed against her, yet she was sent home; and nothing in point of law was done against her'. Thirty years later James Boswell noted, 'It is the fashion of the times to laugh at [witchcraft] as a matter of absurd credulity.'

The superstition was dying, but it was a slow and lingering death. Lawyer and historian Roger North noted the tenacity of the superstition among 'the common ignorants' and wrote, 'It is seldom that a poor wretch is brought to trial upon that account [witchcraft] but there is, at the heels of her, a popular rage that does little less than demand her to be put to death; and, if a judge is so clear and open as to declare against that impious vulgar opinion, that the devil himself has power to torment or kill innocent children, or that he is pleased to divert himself with the good people's cheese, butter, pigs and geese, and the like errors of the ignorant and foolish rabble, the countrymen (the triers) cry, this judge has no religion, for he does not believe in witches, and so, to show they have some, hang the poor wretches.'

The belief lingered longest in rural areas, and nearly two centuries after Hopkins' death, Robert Forby, the rector of Fincham in Norfolk wrote, 'A deeply rooted superstition is not easily eradicated; and at present it appears to bid defiance to the 'march of intellect' which has brushed away much of our rustic simplicity, and effected a prodigious refinement in our persons and manners. The village lass still hoards her sixpence that she may cross the hand of the fortune-teller with silver, and learn the events of her future years: and amongst those of a somewhat higher rank, it is not uncommonly the first thought that occurs to a person who has been robbed, to consult the 'wise woman' or the 'cunning man'. It is, however, a good symptom, that this is seldom done openly. They entertain the belief, but are ashamed to own it; and there may be just grounds to hope that the superstition, which nobody cares to avow, is in a fair way to lose its influence.'

Parson Forby went on to say that belief in witchcraft was 'the only really popular and prevailing instance of superstition existing amongst us; and although not now so triumphant as in the days of Hopkins, the witchfinder general, when sixty witches were hanged in one year in the county of Suffolk; yet still, if the reward of ten pounds were again offered for the discovery of every witch, a sufficient number would be found to furnish a decent income to any modern Hopkins.'

Forby, who died in 1825, noted that many of the ancient remedies continued to be considered effective. Of one such specific he wrote, 'If in the near neighbourhood or anywhere indeed within the malignant influence of a known witch, a child is afflicted with an obstinate ague, a great many worms, or any pining sickness; if a calf be dizzy or a cow 'tail shotten' or have 'gargot' or 'red water' so that it may reasonably be concluded to be bewitched; the most effectual remedy or mode of exorcism is to take a quantity of the patient's urine and boil it with nine nails from as many old horseshoes. The process is to begin exactly at midnight. The conductress of it is to have an assistant to obey orders, but is to touch nothing herself. A single word mars the whole charm. At a certain point in the process, when three, five or seven of the nails have been put in motion at once by the force of the boiling fluid, for some cases are more difficult than others, the spirit is cast out: at which moment the child squalls, the cow 'blores' or the calf 'blares', convalescence immediately commences of course. The good woman from whom the author obtained this valuable information, not immediately, indeed, nor without some little breach of confidence, confirmed it by recounting a failure that once befell herself. She had prevailed on a boy to sit up with her. All was going on most prosperously. The hobnails were in merry motion. The child in the cradle squalled. The boy, in a cold sweat, ventured to look behind him: he was so overpowered with terror that he forgot all the cautions he had received and called to his mistress to look at the little black thing which was endeavouring to escape through the key-hole. This was, no doubt, the evil spirit, which, thus recalled, must have entered the poor child again, for it certainly never recovered.'

Tales of old women making pacts with the Devil and sealing them with their blood, or of sending imps to lame cattle or kill their neighbours were all nonsense. No woman ever copulated with a cloven-footed and hollow-voiced fiend from Hell. No man, woman or child languished and died because they had been 'touched', 'overlooked' or given an apple by a witch (though this is not to say that no 'witch' ever killed a child by poison). No imps in the form of a rabbit called Antony, a crow called Will, a sparrow called Harry or reddish dun mice called Jack and Will killed or sank ships. No beer was ever bewitched by a turkey imp called Great Turkeycock, and no polecat ever interrupted a woman at her spinning wheel and asked her to deny Christ.

Many of those hanged as witches were certainly guilty of cursing their neighbours – a popular imprecation was for 'pox, piles and a heavy vengeance' to afflict the victim. Some old women may have genuinely hoped that their curses would be effective, and may have been deluded into thinking that they really did have the power to injure when one of their curses was followed by a mishap. But the link was coincidental, not supernatural. Some witches admitted having knowledge of herbal healing and were acknowledged within their community as wise women or cunning men, but for most of them the main imperative was to escape hunger and poverty.

John Gaule's tirade against Hopkins was followed by more tracts against the superstition, notably by Sir Robert Filmer who used legal logic to demolish the usual proofs of witchcraft, and Thomas Ady who attacked the 'horrible lies and impossibilities' recorded in books on demonology including those written by Hopkins and King James. Once Hopkins had left the scene the number of witchcraft cases coming before the courts declined dramatically as did the number of executions. In 1649 two old women were hanged for witches in Norwich in the company of eight men who had participated in an anti-Puritan riot, and 'two notorious witches' were hanged at St Albans. Joan Peterson, 'an able practitioner in physic' to some people and 'the witch of Wapping' to others, was hanged at Tyburn in 1652, the same year that six women were executed at Maidstone. Some of them pleaded 'that they were with child pregnant, but confessed it was not by any man but by the Devil.'

A year later old Anne Bodenham was hanged at Salisbury. She had been servant to John Lambe, a physician and dabbler in sorcery who had enjoyed the protection of one of King James's favourites, the Duke of Buckingham. Lambe, who had been blamed by some for causing a violent storm over London, was stoned to death by a mob in 1628 shortly before the murder of his protector. Mistress Bodenham, nicknamed 'Dr Lambe's Darling', retired to a village in Wiltshire where she cultivated a reputation as a wise woman by using some tricks she had picked up from her former employer. She claimed that she could cure illnesses, find stolen property and identify thieves. She was accused of having the ability to 'transform herself into the shape of a mastiff dog, a black lion, a white bear, a wolf, a bull and a cat; and by her charms and spells send either man or woman 40 miles an hour in the air.'

Sensation-seeking pamphleteers, the 17th century's equivalent of today's tabloid press, continued to publish reports of witchcraft trials from around the country and there appeared one linking witchcraft with the recently formed Quakers alleging 'strange and wonderful satanical apparitions, and the appearing of the Devil unto them in the likeness of a black boar, a dog with flaming eyes, and a black man without a head, causing the dogs to bark, the swine to cry, and the cattle to run.' Then later came 'strange and terrible news from Cambridge' of a woman being turned into a bay mare by Quakers who rode her to town and when she resumed her proper likeness and shape 'her sides were all rent and torn, as if they had been spur-galled.'

England's last case of convictions being based on the evidence of hysterical children was at Bury St Edmunds in 1662 in a trial conducted by Sir Matthew Hale who was considered 'one of the brightest luminaries of the law.' Rose Cullender and Amy Duny, two Lowestoft witches who did some occasional baby-sitting, were charged with bewitching children so that they had fits, saw spectres and vomited pins. Amy was presumed to have muttered curses when she had begged for but been refused a few herrings. She had certainly had cause to be angry when farmer John Soam's cart smashed into the side of her house, but he declared that her rantings were witchcraft because the cart then got stuck in a gateway although it did not touch the posts. Evidence that Duny had a teat to feed an imp was accepted although it came from the mother of one of the bewitched girls. Despite ample evidence of fraud and the constant denials of the accused the two widows were condemned.

Amy Duny and Rose Cullender were the last women to be hanged as witches in Suffolk. Those discovered by Matthew Hopkins in Essex and hanged in 1645 were probably the last to die in that county for witchcraft. In Norfolk in 1676 Ellen Julian from Brisley died in Thetford jail while awaiting trial. The last execution in south-east England was probably that of Joan Neville for bewitching to death in 1660.

A quarrel between farmer Joseph Weeden and Ann Foster escalated to arson and a hanging in 1674. He believed she had bewitched his flock of sheep so he used the old method of burning one of the carcases to see if the guilty witch would appear. Ann Foster came along and he cut her with a knife with the idea of ending the bewitchment by shedding her blood. She threatened to sue him for the injury and the quarrel simmered on until some of farmer Weeden's barns and crops went up in smoke. Ann Foster was hanged at Northampton.

England's last witch trials and hangings happened in the West Country. The trial of a Somerset witch in 1664 included rare mention of witches flying on broomsticks. It was said they had used a foul-smelling flying ointment and that one evening 'there came riding three persons upon three broomstaves born up about a yard and a half from the ground.' The last English witches to die were three old women – two widows and a spinster – from Bideford who were hanged in 1682. The evidence involved the familiar themes of old women making nuisances of themselves by their begging, the accused being searched for witch marks, and confessions of sexual relations with the Devil.

Temperance Lloyd was a widow who had faced accusations of witchcraft twice before. She said she had met the Devil in the likeness of a black man with broad eyes and a mouth like a toad, but he was not very big being 'about the length of her arm'. She admitted tormenting people by pricking and pinching them while she was invisible. Susanna Edwards, a pauper widow of 70, said she had met the Devil in the guise of a gentleman dressed all in black and she 'did hope to have a piece of money of him'. Although he had promised that she would 'never want for meat, drink nor clothes', she had continued to live in poverty.

Mary Trembles was a rather weak-willed elderly spinster who fell under Edwards' influence. She confessed that the Devil came to her in the shape of a lion [though she did not know what a lion looked like] and 'had carnal knowledge of her body'. She continued, 'She did go about the town to beg some bread and in her walk did meet with Susanna Edwards who asked her where she had been. Unto whom she answered that she had been about the town and had begged some meat but could get none. Whereupon she together with Susanna Edwards did go to John Barnes's house in hope that there they should have some meat. But he not being within his house they could get no meat or bread being denied by Grace Barnes and her servant who would not give them any meat.'

Soon after refusing to give the two beggar women any food, yeoman's wife, Grace Barnes, was taken ill with 'very great pains of sticking and pricking in her arms, stomach and breast' and she concluded that Edwards and Trembles 'were the very persons that had tormented her by using some magical art or witchcraft upon her body'. Apparently Edwards could inflict the prickings and stabbings with a 'gripe and twinkle of her hands upon her own body' and on one occasion she bewitched a man so that he 'forthwith leapt and capered like a madman and fell a shaking, quivering and foaming, and lay for the space of half an hour like a dying or dead man.' A sailor's wife who also complained of being tormented with pricking pains was told by the doctor that 'it was past his skill to ease her of her pains' and that she was bewitched.

The three women were tried at Exeter in August 1682, declared guilty and condemned to death. The trial judge, Sir Thomas Raymond, described them as 'the most old, decrepit, despicable, miserable creatures that ever he saw. They appeared not only weary of their lives, but to have a great deal of skill to convict themselves.' His opinion was that the evidence was trifling and fanciful, and that the women 'were scarce alive, but were overwhelmed with melancholy and so stupid as no one could suppose they knew either the construction or consequence of what they said.'

Although the executions ceased after 1682 the assize courts continued to hear witchcraft cases. Chief Justice Sir John Holt presided over at least eleven trials and all of them ended in acquittals. One of those cleared as a result of his efforts, though the verdict was unpopular, was Sarah Moreduck who in 1701 was accused of bewitching apprentice Richard Hathaway so that he vomited pins and foamed at the mouth. Thanks to Holt, Hathaway's fraud was revealed and it was he, not the supposed witch, who went to jail. The case was alluded to by a collector of anecdotes who wrote this tale of Judge Holt and his attitude to witchcraft.

'Once when he presided in the Court of King's Bench, a poor, decrepit old creature, equally bowed down by age, poverty and infirmity, was brought before him, charged as a criminal on whom the full severity of the law might be visited with exemplary effect. The terrors of impartiality never sat on any Judge's brow with more impressive dignity or threatening aspect than that of Judge Holt. The trembling culprit was overwhelmed with her fears. The charge was opened. 'What is her crime?' asked his Lordship.

'Witchcraft.'

'And how is it proved?'

'She uses a powerful spell.'

'Let me see it.'

The spell was handed to the bench. It appeared a small ball of variously coloured rags or silk, bound with threads of as many different hues; these were unwound and unfolded until there appeared a scrap of parchment on which were written certain characters now nearly illegible from much use.

'Is this the spell?' The prosecutor averred it was. The Judge, after looking at this potent charm a few minutes, addressed himself to the terrified prisoner: 'Prisoner, how came you by this?'

'A young gentleman, my Lord, gave it me to cure my child's ague.'

'How long since?'

'Thirty years, my Lord.'

'And did it cure her?'

'Oh, yes, and many others.'

'I am glad of it.'

The Judge paused and addressed himself to the jury. 'Gentlemen of the jury, thirty years ago, I and some companions as thoughtless as myself went to this woman's dwelling, then a public house, and after enjoying ourselves, found we had no means to discharge the reckoning. I had recourse to a stratagem: observing a child ill of an ague, I pretended I had a spell to cure her. I wrote the classic line you see on a scrap of parchment, and was discharged of the demand on me by the gratitude of the poor woman before us for the supposed benefit. Nature doubtless did much for the patient, the force of imagination the rest. This incident but ill suits my present character and the station in which I sit, but to conceal it would be to aggravate the folly for which it becomes me to atone, to endanger innocence and encourage superstition.' The verdict may be imagined, and Judge Holt's address at this trial was one of the death blows that he gave to trials for witchcraft.

'Among the many merits won by Chief Justice Holt, we must not forget that of effectually repealing the Acts against witchcraft, although they nominally continued on the statute book to a succeeding reign. Eleven poor creatures were successively tried before him for this supposed crime, and the prosecutions were supported by the accustomed evidence of long fasting, vomiting of pins and ten-penny nails, secret teats sucked by imps, devil's marks, and cures by the sign of the cross, or drawing blood from the sorceress; but by Holt's good sense and tact in every instance, the imposture was detected to the satisfaction of the jury, and there was an acquittal. One of the strongest prima facie cases put before him was years before he had given the cabalistic charm, which was adduced as the chief proof of her guilt. At last, the Chief Justice effectually accomplished his object by directing that a prosecutor who pretended that he had been bewitched should himself be indicted as an impostor and a cheat.

'This fellow had sworn that a spell cast upon him had taken away from him the power of swallowing, and that he had fasted for ten weeks; but the manner in which he had secretly received nourishment was clearly proved. He nevertheless made a stout defence, and numerous witnesses deposed to his expectoration of pins, and his abhorrence of victuals; all which they ascribed to the malignant influence of the witch. The Judge, having extracted from a pretended believer in him the answer that 'All the devils in hell could not have helped him fast so long,' and having proved by cross-examining another witness, that he had a large stock of pins in his pocket, from which those supposed it be vomited were taken, summed up with great acuteness and left it to the jury to say, not whether the defendant was bewitched, but whether he was non compos mentis, or was fully aware of the knavery he was committing, and knowingly wished to impose on mankind. The jury found a verdict of guilty; and the impostor standing in the pillory, to the satisfaction of the whole country, no female was ever after in danger of being hanged or burned for being old, wrinkled and paralytic.'

The last person to be convicted of witchcraft in England was Jane Wenham 'the wise woman of Walkern' in 1712. She was a cantankerous woman with a bad reputation. The vicar tried to put a stop to her feud with a farmer by having him pay a shilling to soothe her feelings but a young servant girl had fits and Jane was accused of witchery. The judge, Sir John Powell, favoured acquittal but the jury said she was guilty. The judge delayed execution and won her a royal pardon and the result was a bout of pamphlet warfare for and against the belief in witchcraft. The *Impossibility of Witchcraft, Plainly Proving From Scripture and Reason That there never was a Witch; and that it is both Irrational and Impious to believe there ever was. In which the Depositions against Jane Wenham, Lately Try'd and Condemned for a Witch at Hertford, are Confuted and Expos'd* was answered by *The Belief of Witchcraft Vindicated; proving from Scripture, there have been Witches, and from Reason, that there be Such still.* The anti-witchcraft writer came back with *The Impossibility of Witchcraft Further Demonstrated. Both from Scripture and Reason* which was again countered by *A Defense of the Proceedings against Jane Wenham, wherein the Possibility and Reality of Witchcraft are Demonstrated from Scripture.*

In 1717 Jane Clerk and her son and daughter were the last persons in England to be charged with witchcraft. They were swum and 'they swam like a cork, a piece of paper or an empty barrel, though they strove all they could to sink.' It was claimed that their victims suffered strange illnesses, and on the advice of a cunning man urine from the afflicted was put in a bottle and corked. It eased the suffering but the 'water would always give a crack like a gun and the cork fly out' and then the pains returned. When the urine was boiled one of the suspects would appear 'sometimes in the shape of a cat and sometimes a dog who would run in panting as if he was upon a hard chase and these dogs and cats would come in though the doors and windows were shut and all passages except the keyholes and chimneys stopped and could never be caught but would grin furiously, and approaching near the bewitched persons give them great pain and so vanish.' Then the cunning man suggested a charm of rosemary, marigolds, ale and blood but it flew out of the house and hit a cow. They tried scratching the old woman but her skin was so tough that they had to hold her down with the aid of a village constable and use 'great pins and such instruments.' Some of the bewitched vomited stones and others had big black bees come out of their noses. Jane Clerk was publicly searched and flesh 'like the teats of an ewe and some like the paps of a cat' were found in her secret parts. But the allegations were rejected and the matter did not come to court.

In June 1736 the witchcraft statutes covering England, Scotland and Wales were scrapped. In Scotland the last execution was in 1727 when senile Janet Horne was burned at Dornoch. Her daughter had supposedly been shod like a horse to fly her mother to witch meetings and lamed by it. The witchcraft laws covering Ireland, which like Wales had been virtually unaffected by the witch-mania, were abolished in 1821.

Still the belief in the old tests of guilt endured, notably weighing against a church bible and swimming. At Coggeshall in Essex in 1699 widow Coman, who by 'common report' was said to be a witch, was swum three times in eleven days in July during a period of persecution led by the village vicar. She was over sixty and obviously demented. Her husband had recently drowned in their well and she kept muttering about butter being eight pence a pound and cheese a groat. The son of the man supposed to have been lamed by her witchcraft drew blood by scratching her with nails and smeared it on his handkerchief which he took home and burned. But the remedy failed. A mob put her in the river 'several times and she always swum like a cork and because the mob was so troublesome to her she said when she was swimming Ye see what I am, what need to swim me any more. Soon after, whether by the cold she got in the water or some other means, she fell very ill and died.' The vicar had the corpse searched 'in the presence of some sober women' and claimed that 'excressencies like to biggs with nipples which seemed as if they had been frequently sucked' were found.

Swimming suspected witches went on long after the abolition of the witch laws. In December 1748 at Monks Eleigh in Suffolk 'Alice, the wife of Thomas Green, labourer, was swum, malicious and evil people having raised an ill report of her being a witch.' In 1751 an old

121

couple died after being stripped, tied and thrown into a muddy stream near Tring and one of the perpetrators was hanged.

In 1792 an 'old woman applied to the Justices of Bury St Edmunds for redress against imputation of witchcraft; but as she was informed that no cognisance could be taken of her case, she returned to her parish with a full determination to pass the common ordeal, and which, as it was solicited on her part, was inflicted by her husband, his brother and another man.' Another report said 'On one of the bricks which are close to the threshold of the door of Stanningfield church, is a glazed tile on which is a figure of a horseshoe, for the purpose it is said of preventing witches from entering the church. However, in spite of this celebrated horseshoe placed where it now is for the protection of the parish, it does not seem to have produced the desired effect, as so late as the year 1795, an unfortunate witch was discovered in Stanningfield and went through the usual sufferings in a pond close by the church.'

Early in the 19th century Norfolk parson Robert Forby described another Suffolk swimming. 'It [belief in witchcraft] is yet far from being extinct amongst us. No longer ago that the summer of 1825, an old man was swum in the presence of a large concourse of people in the parish of Wickham Skeith in Suffolk for the supposed crime of bewitching one of his female neighbours. There was nothing amatory in the case, but much arrant ignorance and superstition. There had been, it seems, a quarrel between the parties respecting a pig; in consequence of which the man had uttered threats or was supposed to harbour revenge. Soon after this, the woman [who was occasionally disturbed in her mind] was seized with odd symptoms and began to exhibit strange vagaries. Amongst other pranks, it was affirmed and believed that she ran up the walls of the room and hung upon the joists or beams in the ceiling like a cat; a feat which, it was unanimously agreed, no one could have performed unless she was possessed.

'It was accordingly decided by wise heads of the parish that the woman was bewitched and that the man had bewitched her. But to put the matter beyond a doubt it was determined to swim him; and this sentence was put in execution in the Grimmer, a large pond upon the village green. And sure enough their suspicions were fully confirmed; for, when he was put into the water he floated like a cork. After many and unavailing efforts to make him sink, which were continued for three quarters of an hour, the poor old man was suffered to escape. But it was not without difficulty that he was rescued from a repetition of the ordeal, by the active interference of the minister and churchwardens of the parish, as soon as it came to their knowledge; and it was with still greater difficulty that the belief of his supernatural power of doing mischief was eradicated from the minds of his neighbours. Great pains were taken for this purpose by the clergyman; but, after all the arguments that could be used, many of them were rather shamed out of the avowal than convinced of the absurdity of the superstition.'

Some years later at Sible Hedingham a man of about 80 who earned a few pennies by fortune-telling died after being swum in a millpond. Some people were sent to prison with the judge saying that a deep belief in witchcraft 'possesses to a lamentable extent the tradespeople and lower orders of the district.' In 1737, a year after the repeal of the witch laws, an old woman from Great Oakley, Bedfordshire, was tested by swimming and weighing against the church bible. First she was swum but the result was uncertain so they weighed her against the church bible. Proving to be considerably heavier than the book she was cleared. Susannah Haynokes of Wingrave in Buckinghamshire was accused of bewitching a neighbour's spinning wheel in 1759. Her husband insisted that she should be tested by weighing and she too turned out to be considerably heavier than the book.

Alice Brown, a young girl from Great Paxton near Huntingdon, fell through the ice on the Great Ouse in 1808 and had fits. An interfering neighbour declared that Alice and her hysterical young friends were under a spell and gossip quickly blamed old Ann Izzard who offered to be put to the church bible test. Although the curate of the parish preached against their 'ignorance, credulity and barbarity', the villagers gathered one Sunday, dragged Ann out of her cottage, pricked her with pins and assaulted her. When she heard that they planned to swim her she fled to another village.

Sailors in the 19th century were sold winds in three magical knots by women in the Orkneys and Shetlands, 'the buyer was told he would get a good gale when he untied the first knot, the second knot would bring a strong wind, and the third a severe tempest.'

There were instances of people being charged with assault when they scratched and drew blood from supposed witches. In 1847 'a complaint was recently lodged before the bench of magistrates at Cromer by a poor woman who was employed in carrying a letter bag along the coast, against some boys who pelted her with stones, and were not satisfied till they had 'drawn blood' as they said, 'from the old witch'. A man who won some sausages in a raffle fell ill after eating them and was persuaded that he was bewitched. He went to a cunning woman in Yarmouth and she gave him a potion and a copy of the Lord's Prayer to wear next to his heart . 'He was also required to send to her some of his hair cut from the nape of the neck, parings of his toe and finger nails and a bottle of his urine. These were to be operated upon by her in order to complete the cure. The man got better and Mrs Mortimer [the cunning woman] demanded another ten shillings which he refused to pay, but finding himself again in declining health he paid the money, after which he recovered and continued well till the death of the old hag. He has since that event felt it necessary to apply to a cunning man at Norwich. The copy of the Lord's Prayer was worn out on his person.'

As Robert Forby had pointed out, there are always some people prepared to cynically profit from the misfortunes of their fellows. There were no legions of 'devil's darlings' trying to overthrow Christendom or bewitch their neighbours' pigs and cows. Heretical witchcraft was invented by the Inquisition and it was sustained by clerics who fostered ridiculous ideas such as 'maids hang some of their hair before the image of St Urban because they would have the rest of their hair grow long and be yellow. Women with child run to church and tie their girdles or shoe latchets about a bell and strike upon the same thrice thinking that the sound thereof hastens their good delivery. To throw up a black chicken in the air will make all tempests to cease, so it be done with the hand of a witch.'

European witch-mania had permeated all the ranks of a superstitious and unscientific society that was slowly emerging from its medieval past. Hopkins' witch-hunts and the European witch-mania [of which the Salem trials in colonial America in 1692 were essentially a part] have been and remain a rich source for stories by novelists and film-makers, but the facts have been much distorted and exaggerated. Fascination with the occult continues and new forms of pagan 'witchcraft' have appeared but they are totally unconnected with the witchcraft heresy of the 16th and 17th centuries. The word pagan was a derisory term meaning 'rustic' or 'country bumpkin' used by Roman Christians to describe unbelievers.

In 1968 the film *Matthew Hopkins – Witchfinder General* was made using some Suffolk locations. In terms of historical accuracy the plot is laughable. Hopkins [played by Vincent Price] is suitably cold and arrogant and he is seduced by Sara Lowes, the supposed niece of Parson Lowes of Brandeston. She gives herself to the witchfinder in the hope that he will spare her gentle and softly spoken uncle [played by Rupert Davies] who is 'swum' in the moat of Kentwell Hall before being hanged there. The most grotesque distortion involves John Stearne. He is portrayed as a drunken, foul-mouthed lecher and rapist who delights in stabbing the marks on his victims' bodies. Elizabeth Clarke, the first victim of the witch-hunt, is shown being lowered into a fire outside Lavenham's Guild Hall and it all ends with Sara's true love, a soldier in Parliament's army, killing Stearne and then hacking at Hopkins with an axe in Orwell Castle before the Witchfinder General is shot and killed.

THE
Discovery of Witches:
IN
Answer to severall QUERIES
LATELY
Delivered to the Judges of Assize for the
County of NORFOLK.
And now published
By MATTHEW HOPKINS, Witch-finder
FOR The Benefit of the whole KINGDOME
EXOD 22.18
Thou shalt not suffer a witch to live.

Certaine queries answered, which have been and are likely to be objected against Matthew Hopkins, in his way of finding out Witches

Querie 1. That he must needs be the greatest Witch, Sorcerer and Wizard himselfe, else hee could not doe it.
Answ. If Satans kingdome be divided against it selfe, how shall it stand?

Querie 2. If he never went so farre as is before mentioned, yet for certaine he met with the Devill, and cheated him of his Booke, wherein were written all the Witches names in England, and if he looks on any witch, he can tell by her countenance what she is; so by this, his helpe is from the Devill.
Answ. If he had been too hard for the devill and got his book, it had been to his great commendation, and no disgrace at all: and for judgement in Phisiognomie, he hath no more than any man else whatsoever.

Quer. 3. From whence then proceed this his skill? Was it from his profound learning, or from much reading of learned Authors concerning that subject?

Answ. From neither of both, but from experience, which though it be meanly esteemed of, yet the surest and safest way to judge by.

Quer .4. I pray where was this experience gained? And why gained by him and not by others?

Answ. The Discoverer never travelled far for it, but in March 1644 [1645] he had some seven or eight of that horrible sect of Witches living in the Towne where he lived, a Towne in Essex called Maningtree, with divers other adjacent Witches of other towns, who every six weeks in the night (being alwayes on the Friday night) had their meeting close by his house, and had their severall solemne sacrifices there offered to the Devill, one of which this discoverer heard speaking to her Imps one night, and bid them goe to another Witch, who was thereupon apprehended, and searched by women who had many yeares knowne the Devills marks, and found to have three teats about her, which honest women have not: so upon command from the Justice, they were to keep her from sleep two or three nights, expecting in that time to see her familiars, which the fourth night she called in by their severall names, and told them what shapes, a quarter of an houre before they came in, there being ten of us in the roome; the first she called was,

1 Holt, who came in like a white kitling.

2 Jarmara, who came in like a fat Spaniel without any legs at all, she said she kept him fat, for she clapt her hand on her belly, and said he suckt good blood from her body.

3 Vinegar Tom, who was like a long-legg'd Greyhound, with an head like an Oxe, with a long taile and broad eyes, who when this discoverer spoke to, and bade him goe to the place provided for him and his Angels, immediately transformed himselfe into the shape of a child of foure yeeres old without a head, and gave halfe a dozen turnes about the house, and vanished at the doore.

4 Sack and Sugar, like a black Rabbet.

5 Newes, like a Polcat. All these vanished away in a little time. Immediately after this Witch confessed severall other Witches, from whom she had her Imps, and named to divers women where their marks were, the number of their Marks, and Imps, and Imps names, as Elemanzer, Pyewacket, Peckin the Crown, Grizzel Greedigut, &c., which no mortall could invent; and upon searches the same Markes were found, the same number, and in the same place, and the like confessions from them of the same Imps,

127

(though they knew not that we were told before) and so peached one another thereabouts that joyned together in the like damnable practise, that in our Hundred in Essex, 29 were condemned once, 4 brough 25 Miles to be hanged, where this Discoverer lives, for sending the Devill like a Beare to kill him in his garden, so by seeing diverse of the Papps, and trying wayes with hundreds of them, he gained this experience, and for ought he knowes any man else may find them as well as he and his company, if they had the same skill and experience.

Quer. 5. Many poore people are condemned for having a Pap or Teat about them, whereas many People (especially antient People) are and have been a long time troubled with naturall wretts on severall parts of their bodies, and other naturall excressencies as Hemerodes, Piles, Childbearing, &c. And these shall be judged on by one man alone, and a woman, and so accused or acquitted.

Answ. The parties so judging can justifie their skill to any, and shew good reasons why such markes are not meerly naturall, neither that they can happen by any such naturall cause as is before expressed, and for further answer for their private judgements alone, it is most false and untrue, for never was any man tryed by search of his body, but commonly a dozen of the ablest men in the parish or else where, were present, and most commonly as many ancient skilfull matrons and midwives present when the women were tryed, which marks not only he, and his company attest to be very suspitious, but all beholders, the skilfulest of them, doe not approve of them, but likewise assent that such tokens cannot in their judgements proceed from any of the above mentioned Causes.

Quer. 6. It is a thing impossible for any man or woman to judge rightly on such marks, they are neare to naturall excressencies, and they that finde them, durst not presently give Oath they were drawne by evill spirits, till they have used unlawfull courses of torture to make them say anything for ease and quiet, as who would not do? but I would know the reasons he speakes of and how and whereby to discover the one from the other and so be satisfied in that.

Answ. The reasons in breefe are three, which for the present he judgeth to differ from naturall marks; which are: He judgeth by the unusualnes of the place where he findeth the teats in or on their bodies, being farre distant from any usuall place from whence

128

such naturall markes proceed, as if a witch plead the markes found are Emerods, if J finde them on the bottome of the back-bone, shall J also be with him, knowing they are not neere that veine, and so others by childbearing, when it may be they are in the contrary part?

2. They are most commonly insensible, and feele neither pin, needle, aule, &c, thrust through them.

3. The often variations and mutations of these marks into severall formes, confirmes the matter, as if a Witch hear a month or two before that the Witch-finder (as they call him) is comming, they will, and have put out their Imps to others to suckle them, even to their owne young and tender children; these upon search are found to have dry skinnes and filmes only, and be close to the flesh, keepe her 24 houres with a diligent eye, that none of her spirits come in any visible shape to suck her; the women have seen the next day after her Teats extended out of their former filling length, full of corruption ready to burst, and leaving her alone then one quarter of an houre, and let the women go up againe, and shee will have them drawn by her Imps close againe: Probatum est. Now for answer to their tortures in its due place.

Quer. 7. How can it possibly be that the Devill being a spirit, and wants no nutriment or sustenation, should desire to suck any blood? and indeed as he is a spirit he cannot draw any such excressences, having neither flesh nor bone, nor can be felt, &c.
Answ. He seekes not their bloud, as if he could not subsist without that nourishment, but he often repairs to them, and gets it, the more to aggravate the Witches damnation, and to put her in mind of her Covenant: and as he is a Spirit and Prince of the ayre, he appeares to them in any shape whatsoever, which shape is occasioned by him through joyning of condensed thickned aire together, and many times doth assume shapes of many creatures; but to create any thing he cannot do it, it is only proper to God: But in this case of drawing out of these Teats, he doth really enter into the body, reall, corporeall, substantiail creature, and forceth that Creature (he working in it) to his desired ends, and useth the organs of that body to speake withall to make his compact up with the Witches, be the creature Cat, Rat, Mouse, &c.

Quer. 8. When these Paps are fully discovered, yet that will not serve sufficiently to convict them, but they must be tortured and kept from sleep two or three nights, to distract them, and make them say any thing; which is a way to tame a wilde Colt or Hawke, &c.

Ans. In the infancy of this discovery it was not only thought fitting, but enjoyned in Essex and Suffolke by the Magistrates, with this intention only, because they being kept awake would be more the active to cal their Imps to open view the sooner to their helpe, which often times have so happened; and never or seldome did any Witch ever complain in the time of their keeping for want of rest, but after they had beat their heads together in the Goale; and after this use was not allowed of by the Judges and other Magistrates, it was never since used, which is a yeare and a halfe since, neither were any kept from sleep by any order or direction since; but peradventure their owne stubborne wills did not let them sleep, though tendered and offered to them.

Quer. 9. Beside that unreasonable watching, they were extraordinarily walked, till their feet were blistered, and so forced through that cruelty to confesse, &c.

Ans. It was in the same beginning of this discovery, and the meaning of walking of them at the highest extend of cruelty, was only they to walke about themselves the night they were watched, only to keepe them waking: and the reason was this, when they did lye or sit in a chaire, if they did offer to couch downe, then the watchers were only to desire them to sit up and walke about, for indeed when they be suffered so to couch, immediately comes their Familiars into the room and scareth the watchers, and heartneth on the Witch, though contrary to the true meaning of the same instructions, diverse have been by rusticall People, (they hearing them confess to be Wicches) mis-used, spoiled, and abused, diverse whereof have suffered for the same, and could never be proved against this Discoverer to have a hand in it, or consent to it; and hath likewise been un-used by him and others, ever since the time they were kept from sleepe.

Quer. 10. But there hath been an abominable, inhumane, and unmerciful tryall of these poore creatures, by tying them, and heaving them into the water; a tryall not allowable by Law or conscience, and I would faine know the reasons for that.

Ans. It is not denyed but many were so served as had Papps, and floated, others that had none were tryed with them and sunk, but marke the reasons.

For first the Divels policie is great, in perswading many to come of their owne accord to be tryed, perswading them their marks are so close they shall not be found out, so as diverse have come 10 or 12 Miles to be searched of their own accord, and hanged for their labour (as one Meggs a Baker did, who lived within 7 Miles of Norwich, and was hanged at Norwich Assizes for witchcraft) then when they find that the Devil tells them false they reflect on him, and he (as 40 have confessed) adviseth them to be sworne, and tels them they shall sinke and be cleared that way, then when they be tryed that way and floate, they see the Devill deceives them againe, and have so laid open his treacheries.

2. It was never brought in against any of them at their tryals as any evidence.

3. King James in his Demonology saith, it is a certaine rule for (saith he) Witches deny their baptisme when they Covenant with the Devill, water being the sole element thereof, and therefore saith he, when they be heaved into the water, the water refuseth to receive them into her bosome, (they being such Miscreants to deny their baptisme) and suffers them to float, as the Froath on the Sea, which the water will not receive, but casts it up and downe, till it comes to the earthy element the shore, and there leaves it to consume.

4. Observe these generation of Witches, if they be at any time abused by being called Whore, Theefe, &c, by any where they live, they are the readiest to cry and wring their hands, and shed tears in abundance, & run with full and right sorrowfull acclamations to some Justice of Peace, and with many teares make their complaints: but now behold their stupidity; nature or the elements reflection from them, when they are accused for this horrible and damnable sin of Witchcraft, they never alter or change their countenances, nor let one Teare fall. This (....) she was, swimming (by able Divines whom I reverence) is condemned for no way, and therefore of late hath, and for ever shall be left.

Quer. 11. Oh! But if this torturing Witch-catcher can by all or any of these meanes, wring out a word or two of confession from any of these stupified, ignorant, unitelligible, poore silly creatures, (though none heare it but himselfe) he will adde and put her in feare to confesse telling her, else she shall be hanged; but if she doe, he will set her at liberty, and so put a word into her mouth, and make such a silly creature confesse she knowes not what.

Answ. He is of a better conscience, and for your better understanding of him, he doth thus uncase himselfe to all, and declares what confessions (though made by a Witch against her selfe) he allows not of, and doth altogether account of no validity, or worthy of credence to be given to it, and ever did so account it, and ever likewise shall.

1. He utterly denyes that confession of a Witch to be of any validity, when it is drawn from her by any torture or violence whatsoever; although after watching, walking, or swimming, diverse have suffered, yet peradvanture Magistrates with much care and diligence did solely and fully examine them after sleepe, and consideration sufficient.

2. He utterly denyes that confession of a Witch, which is drawn from her by flattery, viz. If you will confesse you shall go home, you shall not go to the Gaole, nor be hanged &c.

3. He utterly denyes that confession of a Witch, when she confesseth any improbability, impossibility, as flying in the ayre, riding on a broom &c.

4. He utterly denyes a confession of a Witch, when it is interrogated to her, and words put into her mouth, to be of any force or effect: as to say to a silly (yet Witch wicked enough) you have foure Imps, have you not? She answers affirmatively, Yes: did they not suck you? Yes, saith she: Are not their names so and so? Yes saith shee: Did not you send such an Impe to kill my child? Yes saith she, this being all her confession after this manner, it is by him accompted nothing and he earnestly doth desire that all Magistrates and Jurors would a little more then ever they did, examine witnesses, about the interrogation confessions.

Quer. 12. If all these confessions be denyed, I wonder what he will make a confession, for sure it is, all these wayes have been used and took for good confessions, and many have suffered for them, and I know not what, he will then make a confession.

Answ. Yes, in brief he will declare what confession of a Witch is of validity and force in his judgement, to hang a Witch: when a Witch is first found with teats, then sequestred from her house, which is onely to keep her old associates from her, and so by good counsell brought into a sad condition, by understanding of the horribleness of her sin, and the judgements threatened against her; and knowing the Devills malice and subtile circumventions. Is brought to remorse and sorrow for complying with Satan so

132

long, and disobeying Gods sacred Commands, doth then desire to unfold her mind with much bitterness, and then without any of the before-mentioned hard usages or questions put to her, doth of her owne accord declare what was the occasion of the Devils appearing to her, whether ignorance, pride, anger, malice, &c, was predominant over her, she doth then declare what speech they had, what likeness he was in, what voice he had, what familiars he sent her, what number of spirits, what names they had, what shabe they were in, what imployment she set them about to severall persons in severall places, (unknowne to the hearers) all wich mischiefs being proved to be done, at the same time she confessed to the same parties for the same cause, and all effected, is testimony enough against her for all her denyall.

Quest. 73. How can any possible beleeve that the Devill and the Witch joyning together, should have such power, as the Witches confesse, etc.kill such and such a man, child, horse, cow, or the like; if we beleeve they can doe what they will, then we derogate from Gods power, who for certain limits the Devill and the Witch; and I cannot beleeve they have any power at all.

Answ. God suffers the Devill many times to doe much hurt, and the devill doth play many times the deluder and imposter with these Witches, in perswading them that they are the cause of such and such a murder wrought by him with their consents, when and indeed neither he nor they had any hand in it, as thus: We must needs argue, he is of a long standing, above 6000 yeers, then he must needs be the best Scholar in all knowledges of arts and tongues, & so have the best skill in Physicke, judgement in Physiognomie, and knowledge of what disease is reigning or predominant in this or that mans body, (and so for cattell too) by reason of his long experience. This subtile tempter knowing such a man lyable to some sudden disease (as by experience I have found) as Plurisie, Imposthume, &c. he resorts to divers Witches, if they know the man, and seek to make a difference between the Witches and the party, it may be by telling them he hath threatned to have them very shortly searched, and so hanged for Witches, then they all consult with Satan to save themselves, and Satan stands ready prepared, with a (The Devills speech to the Witches) What will you have me doe for you, my deare and nearest children, covenanted and compacted with me in my hellish league, and sealed with your blood, my delicate firebrand-darlings. Oh thou (say they) that at the first didst promise to save us thy servants from any of our deadly enemies discovery, and didst promise to avenge and slay all those, we pleased, that did offend us; Murther that wretch suddenly who threatens the down-fall of your loyall subjects. He then promiseth to effect it. Next newes is heard the partie is dead, he comes to the witch, and gets a world of reverence, credence and respect for his power and activeness, when and indeed the disease kills the party, not the Witch, nor the Devill, (onely the Devill knew that such a disease was predominant) and the witch aggravates her damnation by her familiarity and consent to the Devill and so comes likewise in compass of the Lawes. This is Satans usuall impostring and deluding, but not his constant course of procedding, for he and the witch doe mischiefe too much. But I would that Magistrates and Jurats would a little examine witnesses when they heare witches confess such and such a murder, whether the party had not long time before, or at the time when the witch grew suspected, some disease or other predominant, which might cause that issue or effect of death.

Quer. 14. All that the witch-finder doth, is to fleece the country of their money, and therefore rides and goes to townes to have imployment, and promiseth them faire promises, and it may be doth nothing for it, and possesseth many men that they have so many wizzards and so many witches in their towne, and so hartens them on to entertaine him.

Ans. You doe him a great deal of wrong in every of these particulars. For first,
1. He never went to any towne or place, but they rode, writ, or sent often for him, and were (for ought he knew) glad of him.
2. He is a man that doth disclaime that ever he detected a witch, or said, Thou are a witch; only after her tryall by search, and their owne confessions, he as others may judge.
3. Lastly, judge how he fleeceth the Country, and inriches himselfe, by considering the vast summe he takes of every towne, he demands but 20.s. a town, & doth sometimes ride 20 miles for that, & hath no more for all his charges thither and back again (& it may be stayes a weeke there) and finde there 3 or 4 witches, or if it be but one, cheap enough, and this is the great summe he takes to maintaine his Companie with 3 horses.
JUDICET ULLUS.

Select Bibliography

Ady, Thomas, A Candle in the Dark [1656]

Ainsworth, William Harrison, The Lancashire Witches [1848]

Forby, Robert, The Vocabulary of East Anglia [1830]

Baxter, Richard, The Certainty of the World of Spirits [1691]

Bernard, Richard, A Guide to Grand Jurymen [1627]

Davies, Reginald Trevor, Four Centuries of Witch-Beliefs [1947]

Deacon, Richard, Matthew Hopkins: Witch-finder General [1976]

Filmer, Sir Robert, An Advertisement to the Jurymen of England Touching Witches [London 1653]

Ewen, Cecil L'Estrange, The Trials of John Lowes [1937], Witchcraft in the Star Chamber [1938], Witch Hunting and Witch Trials [1929]

Gaule, John, Select Cases of Conscience Touching Witches and Witchcraft [1646]

Glanvill, Joseph, Sadducismus Triumphatus [1681]

Hope Robbins, Rossell, The Encyclopaedia of Witchcraft and Demonology [1959]

Hutchinson, Francis, An Historical Essay Concerning Witchcraft [1718]

King James I, Daemonologie [1597]

Kittredge, George Lyman, Witchcraft in Old and New England [1929]

Potts, Thomas, The Wonderful Discovery of the Witches in the County of Lancaster [1613]

Scot, Reginald, The Discoverie of Witchcraft [1584]

Sprenger, Jakob and Heinrich Kramer, Malleus Maleficarum [1486, translated Montague Summers 1928]

Stearne, John, A Confirmation and Discovery of Witchcraft [1648]

Summers, Montague, The Geography of Witchcraft [1927], The History of Witchcraft and Demonology [1926]

Trevor-Roper, Hugh, The European Witch-craze of the Sixteenth and Seventeenth Centuries [1969]

Also numerous contemporary pamphlets etc. such as A Detection of Damnable Drifts Practised by Three Witches Arraigned at Chelmsford [1579], A true and just Record of the Information, Examination and Confession of all the Witches taken at St Osees in the county of Essex [1582], The Confession of Mother Lakeland of Ipswich [1645], A True Relation of the Arraignment of eighteen witches [1645]

Some quotations contain words or phrases which whilst they were in common use when written, are no longer socially acceptable.
The author and publisher of this book in no way condone their use in a modern context